NATIONAL GEOGRAPHIC

OUR WORLD

STUDENT'S BOOK 4

SERIES EDITORS

JoAnn (Jodi) Crandall
Joan Kang Shin

AUTHOR

Kate Cory-Wright

NATIONAL
GEOGRAPHIC
LEARNING

CENGAGE
Learning·

Australia • Brazil • Japan • Korea • Mexico • Singapore • Spain • United Kingdom • United States

NATIONAL GEOGRAPHIC

OUR WORLD

Let's sing! TR: B45

This is our world.
Everybody's got a song to sing.
Each boy and girl.
This is our world!

I say 'our', you say 'world'.
Our!
World!
Our!
World!

I say 'boy', you say 'girl'.
Boy!
Girl!
Boy!
Girl!

I say everybody move ...
I say everybody stop ...
Everybody stop!

This is our world.
Everybody's got a song to sing.
Each boy and girl.
This is our world!

All in Our Family

In this unit, I will …
- describe physical appearance.
- describe emotions.
- talk about plans.
- write a diary entry.

Look and answer.

1. What is the girl holding?

2. What is she wearing?

3. Who are the other people in the photo?

1 Listen and read. TR: A2

2 Listen and repeat. TR: A3

Hi, I'm Andrea. Here we are at the Martin family picnic. All my **relatives** are here. We're a big family. Some of us look the same. Some of us are very **different**. Our pets are different, too. My cousin thinks my dog, Roxy, is **uglier** than his dog Max. But Roxy is **nicer**. Roxy is also **cleverer** and **friendlier**.

bigger

smaller

stronger

older

younger

taller

shorter

faster

slower

3 **What did you learn?** How are the people different? Discuss with a friend.

Which dog is friendlier?

Roxy is friendlier.

4 Listen, read and sing. TR: A4

We're All Different

I'm taller than you.
He's taller than me.
We're all different.
Yes, we're different.
And I like being me!

My dad is shorter than your dad.
Your brother's taller than mine.
My sister is older than yours.
Your sister's younger than mine.

CHORUS

My horse is bigger than that one.
That horse is smaller than mine.
My horse is funnier than that horse.
It's happy all the time.

CHORUS

5 Work with a friend.
Talk about you. Take turns.

> you / I
>
> my dad / your dad
>
> our car / your car
>
> my pet / your pet

Your dad is tall_____,

but _my dad is taller_____.

8

GRAMMAR TR: A5

My best friend is **bigger** than I am.   I'm **shorter** than he is.
My dog is **friendlier** than my sister's cat.   My dog is **nicer** than her cat.

6 **Read.** Complete the sentences. Use the correct form of the word in brackets.

1. My brother Mun-Hee is _____bigger_____ (big) than I am.

2. My older sister is _____ (friendly) than my little brother.

3. My Aunt Mae-Ran is _____ (clever) than my uncle.

4. My grandmother is _____ (short) than my mother.

5. My cousin Shin is _____ (nice) than me.

6. My cat is _____ (pretty) than your dog.

7 **Work in a group.** Take turns. How are you and your relatives different?

I am taller than my cousin, and stronger, too.

And I'm smaller than my cousins.

8 **Write.** Now compare the people in your group. Use words from the box.

old	short	small	strong	tall	young

_____

_____

_____

_____

_____

9 **Listen and repeat.** Look at the pictures. Match. TR: A6

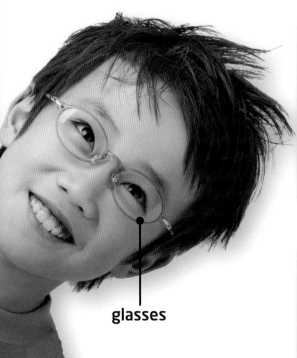

glasses

wavy hair

blonde hair

straight hair

curly hair

1. She looks just like her mother.

2. My cousin is really nice.

3. My cousins are very different.

4. My brother's got blue eyes like me.

a. But he wears glasses, and I don't.

b. They've both got straight hair.

c. I love his wavy hair.

d. But they've both got curly hair.

10 **Listen and stick.** Work with a friend. Talk about you. TR: A7

He's got brown hair.
I've got brown hair, too.

She wears glasses.
I don't!

1 2 3 4 5

What **are** you **doing** on Saturday?
What **are** they **doing** at 7.00?

I'**m going** to my family reunion.
They'**re having** dinner with their neighbours.

11 **Read.** Complete the sentences. Use the correct form of the word in brackets.

1. What's your Aunt Sonia preparing for the reunion on Saturday?

   She _____ (make) her famous chocolate cake.

2. Are you doing something special at the reunion?

   I _____ (run) in the three-legged race, and I

   _____ (eat) lots of chocolate cake.

3. What are you doing for your grandmother's birthday next week?

   I _____ (give) her a card and a box of chocolates.

12 **Play a game.** Cut out the cards on page 161. Play with a friend. Listen, talk and act it out.

Guess what I'm doing after lunch?

After lunch you're playing football.

Where Do Your Eyes Come From?

The colour of our eyes and our hair are family traits. How tall we are, how big or small we are and the shape of our face are all family traits. We say that we inherit these traits from our parents.

Look around you. Many people have got the same colour eyes or colour of hair, but they all look different. It's the special combination of all of these common traits that makes us special. No one else has the same combination of traits as we do.

Are your earlobes attached to the side of your face? Or do they hang free?

How do you fold your hands? Do you cross your right thumb over your left thumb? Or do you cross your left thumb over your right thumb?

It's fun to look for these traits with your family and friends. Try it!

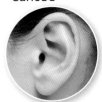
unattached earlobe

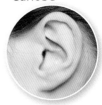
attached earlobe

right thumb over left thumb

EYE COLOUR		
most common		⬛
second most common	⬛	⬛
rarest		⬛

14

14 **Read.** Tick **T** for *True* or **F** for *False*.

1. Eye colour is not a family trait.   Ⓣ Ⓕ

2. All people with black hair look alike.   Ⓣ Ⓕ

3. No one has the same combination of traits you have.   Ⓣ Ⓕ

4. We have got the same traits as our family.   Ⓣ Ⓕ

15 **Work with a friend.** Choose three traits. Who did you inherit these traits from? Discuss.

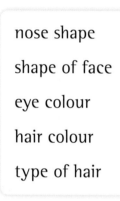

nose shape

shape of face

eye colour

hair colour

type of hair

I've got a long face. I inherited it from my mother. Her face is very long.

People with blonde hair have more hairs on their heads than people with brown hair.

16 **Do a class survey.** Survey your class. How do you fold your hands? Who has got attached earlobes? Record the information on the bar chart.

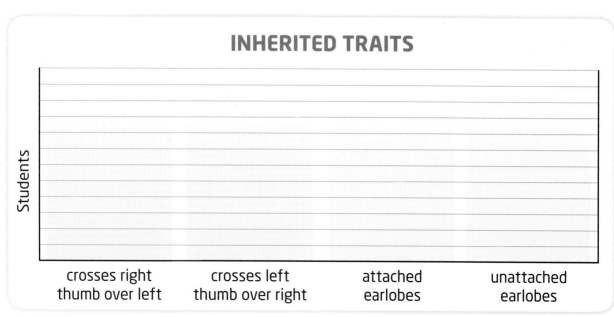

INHERITED TRAITS

Students

crosses right thumb over left   crosses left thumb over right   attached earlobes   unattached earlobes

Diary Entries

In a diary, you write about things that happen in your life and how they make you feel.

17 **Read the diary entry.** What emotions does the writer describe? Underline the emotion words.

4th September

Today was my first day in my new class. I go to a big school, and some of my classmates are new every year. It's nice to meet new friends, but I'm always a little worried and scared at first. Today a girl with curly brown hair smiled at me. A boy with black hair and glasses asked my name. All the children in my class were friendlier than I expected. They made me feel happy to be there. My old friend Sam was there, too. Now he's taller than me. But I don't care. I think I'm cleverer! He thinks this class is harder than our last class. But I think it's more fun. I'm happy to be back at school.

18 **Write.** Write a diary entry about a day in your life. Describe things that happened and how they made you feel.

19 **Work in groups of three.** Share your writing. Take turns. Listen and complete the table.

Name	Event	Emotions

Mission

Understand the human family.

'*Everyone alive today descends from one woman who lived around 180,000 years ago.*'

Spencer Wells, Geneticist
Explorer-in-Residence

- Are all the people in the world one big family? Work in a small group. Discuss.

- How can you learn more about the human family? Why is it important to understand how we are the same and how we are different? Discuss and write the best ideas in the box.

We can research our family tree.

- Work with another group. Share your ideas. Are they the same or different? Which ideas does everyone like best?

20 **Make a class Big Book on family features.**

1. Find a photo of your family and talk to your family about physical characteristics you share.

   • Who in your family has got eyes like yours?
   • Who has got hair like you?
   • Who has got the same mouth as you?
   • Who has got the same nose as you?

2. Work in groups of four to make a Big Book page.

3. Divide the page into four parts.

4. Glue your picture in one of the four parts.

5. Write the names of relatives that you look like.

Now I can ...

- ○ describe physical appearance.
- ○ describe emotions.
- ○ talk about plans.
- ○ write a diary entry.

Here I am. I've got brown eyes. I get my brown eyes from my dad.

19

Fresh Food

In this unit, I will …
• talk about obligation.
• describe frequency.
• discuss and order food.
• express my opinion.

Tick T for *True* or F for *False*.

1. These people are buying vegetables. **T** **F**

2. They are on boats. **T** **F**

3. The vegetables are fresh. **T** **F**

Floating market, Damnoen Saduak, Thailand

1 Listen and read. TR: A10

2 Listen and repeat. TR: A11

Every week people go to the supermarket to buy vegetables like **green beans** and **cucumbers** that come from big farms. Some supermarkets also sell fruit and vegetables from small local farms. But most people think food from the garden is fresher and tastes better than food from a supermarket.

Some lucky people have space to **grow** food in their own gardens. For example, they grow carrots, **onions** and **cabbages**. Many other people do not have space at home, but sometimes they work together to grow food in an allotment.

It's easier than you think to grow vegetables. First you **dig**. Then you **plant** the seeds. But remember to **water** the plants! And you have to **weed** the garden sometimes. When the vegetables are **ripe**, they are **ready to pick**.

dig

plant

water

weed

pick

a pumpkin

a lettuce

a cucumber

a cabbage

chillies

an onion

an aubergine

green beans

a courgette

3 **Work with a friend.** What did you learn? Ask and answer.

Why do people grow their own vegetables?

Because they taste fresher!

23

4 **Listen, read and sing.** TR: A12

Something's Growing

Pumpkin, lettuce, chillies and beans.
Something's growing and it's green.
Pumpkin, lettuce, chillies and beans.
Something's growing and it's green.

Working in the garden,
working in the sun,
working in the garden is a lot of fun.

I have to water the garden.
I have to weed and dig.
I look after my garden.
Those weeds grow very big!

Pumpkin, lettuce, chillies and beans.
Something's growing and it's green.
Pumpkin, lettuce, chillies and beans.
Something's growing and it's green.

We can pick cabbage in the garden.
We can pick some green beans, too.
We can plant carrots in the garden.
I like gardening, don't you?

CHORUS

Pumpkin, lettuce, chillies and beans.
Something's growing and it's green.
Pumpkin, lettuce, chillies and beans.
Something's growing and it's green.

5 **Work with a friend.** Ask and answer.

1. What are three things you can pick?
2. What are two things that you have to do in the garden?

24

I **have to** water the vegetables every day.

I **don't have to** buy any more seeds.

She **has to** plant the tomatoes in a sunny place.

She **doesn't have to** weed today.

6 **Read.** Complete the sentences.

1. I ___have to___ plant these seeds this week.

2. My brother is stronger than me, so he _____ dig.

3. Luisa _____ weed the garden today.

4. My mum _____ water the plants at home.

5. Farmers often _____ buy new seeds.

6. He _____ pick tomatoes this week.

7 **Work with a friend.** Look and make sentences.

8 **What about you?** Write five things you usually have to do.

In the morning I _____.

In the afternoon I _____.

In the evening I _____.

At the weekend I _____.

On Sunday I _____.

9 **Work in a group.** Take turns. Compare what you have to do.

What do you have to do in the morning?

I have to walk my little brother to the bus stop.

10 **Listen and say.** Read and write about what you do. TR: A14

How often?

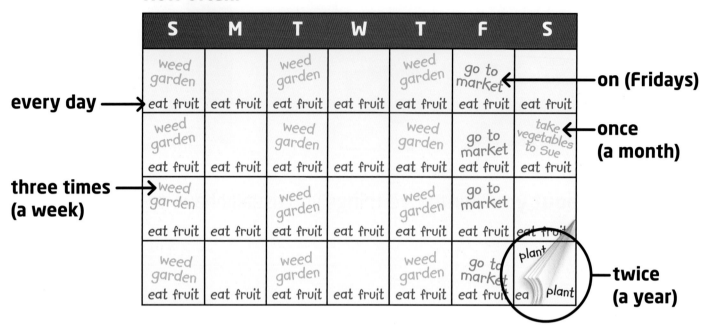

1. Every day I _____.

2. On Fridays I _____.

3. Three times a week I _____.

4. Twice a year I _____.

5. Once a month I _____.

11 **Work with a friend.** Ask and answer, then stick.

How often do you ride your bike?

Twice a day.

What **would** you **like** for lunch?   I'**d like** a bowl of vegetable soup.

12 **Read.** Complete the dialogue.

A: Welcome to Mario's Café. What _____would you like_____ to order today?

B: I _____ some pumpkin soup and courgette bread.

C: I _____ some chicken and rice, please.

D: I usually order cake, but today I _____ some ice cream.

13 **Play a game.** Play with a friend. Make sentences. Take turns.

 Heads: Move 1 space.   Tails: Move 2 spaces.

EVERY DAY

THREE TIMES

TWICE

ON MONDAYS

ON SATURDAYS

ONCE

Where's Your Food From?

Some fruits and vegetables travel a long way to get to your table. Thanks to different kinds of transport, you can enjoy watermelon or strawberries any time of the year. But many people prefer to eat local food from allotments or local farms.

These small local farms produce fruit, vegetables and grains. Some of them also raise animals for milk and meat. People can have fresher food because these farmers grow it locally.

What about cities? There isn't much space to have farms. One way to grow food in a city is on a roof! In this roof garden, a class of children grew 453 kilograms (1,000 pounds) of vegetables in one year. The children grew cabbages, carrots, lettuces and even strawberries! They had to water the plants and weed them, but they enjoyed the food they grew in their outside classroom.

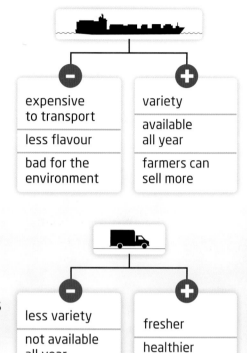

−	+
expensive to transport	variety
less flavour	available all year
bad for the environment	farmers can sell more

−	+
less variety	fresher
not available all year	healthier
may be more expensive	good for local economy

15 Read. Make complete sentences.

1. Some fruits and vegetables   a. in cities.
2. It is very expensive to   b. travel a long way.
3. Food from local farmers   c. is rooftop gardens.
4. There are no small farms   d. transport fresh food.
5. In cities, a way to get to fresh food   e. is fresher and better.

16 Complete the table. Read the problem. Write the solution.

Problem	Solution
There is no local food in winter.	
Transporting food is expensive.	
There is no space to grow food in cities.	

17 Work with a friend. Talk about producing food.
Use these words.

food	fresh	grow	local	meat	plants	raise

Farmers grow most of the food we eat.

Food from local farms is fresh.

Most people spend about five years of their life eating.

31

Paragraphs of Opinion

In a paragraph of opinion, you express your opinion about something. You give the reasons why you feel this way. You can also use words and expressions that introduce your opinion, such as *I think*, *in my opinion* and *I believe*.

18 **Read.** How does the writer introduce opinions? Underline the words and expressions.

Fresh food or tinned food?

When you shop for food, you can buy fresh food or tinned food. Which is better? I think fresh food tastes better. Fresh food is good for you. It does not have any extra salt or sugar. You know just what you are eating. But you have to wash it first because sometimes it is a bit dirty.

There are some positive and negative things about tinned foods, too. In my opinion, tinned food is more convenient because it lasts longer than fresh food. Also, with tinned food you can always have fruit and vegetables – even in winter. But tinned food usually has extra salt or sugar and I believe this is bad for you. Also, tinned foods make more rubbish because you have to throw the tins away.

I think fresh foods are better than tinned foods.

19 **Write.** Write about food from supermarkets and food from local farms. Describe some positive points and some negative points about each one. Express your opinion.

20 **Work in a small group.** Share your writing. Listen and make notes. Write down the names and opinions of your classmates.

Mission

Appreciate local food.

- Which foods can you buy locally? Why is it important to appreciate local food? Work in a small group. Discuss.

- How can you show you appreciate local food? Discuss and write the best ideas in the box.

'*Learning how to grow jalapeños changed my life.*'

Juan Martinez
Environmentalist
Emerging Explorer

Buy food from your local farm.

_____

_____

_____

_____

- Work with another group. Share your ideas. Are they the same or different? Which ideas does everyone like best?

Jalapeño

21 **Make plant cards.**

1. Research a plant you want to grow.

2. Create a card that tells about it. Include a picture and text.

3. Present your plant card to a group.

4. Say why you think your class should grow your plant.

5. Vote for plants to grow in class.

Did you know that a tomato is really a fruit?

This is a tomato plant. Tomato plants have to have lots of sun but they produce lots of tomatoes. And tomatoes are great on pizza!

A Long Time Ago and Today

In this unit, I will …
- describe what people did in the past.
- talk about what the past was like.
- compare the past and the present.
- write a unified paragraph.

Look and circle.

1. This photo is
    a. from the past.   b. from the present.

2. They are riding
    a. to school.   b. to the market.

3. The boy is holding
    a. a box.   b. a computer.

Father and son cycling to school, Uttar Pradesh, India

2 **Listen and repeat.** TR: A18

How did people **spend time** long ago?
Their **life** was different from ours.

Then

How did a typical day **begin**? It began when the sun came up! There were no **electric lights**, so people did all their **housework** during the day. Mothers taught their daughters how to cook, **make** soap, **do the washing up** and **sew** clothes. Fathers taught their sons to make useful **things** for the house, garden or market in **town**. Some children moved away from home to **learn** a craft or trade by working as apprentices.

make soap

Then

fire

At night, families used candles or sat by the **fire**. They didn't have **mobile phones**, TV or **computer games**. They liked playing cards, playing guessing games or **telling** stories until it was time for bed.

3 **Work with a friend.** What did you learn? Ask and answer.

Why did people get up with the sun?

They wanted to do their housework in the daytime. They didn't have electric lights.

sew clothes

Now

do the washing up

tell stories

Now

an electric light

a mobile phone

computer game

39

4 Listen, read and sing. TR: A19

Yesterday and Today

*Things were different a long time ago,
different in so many ways.
Things were different a long time ago,
different from today.*

*A long time ago, children walked to school,
but today I ride my bike.
A long time ago, we learnt to sew our own clothes,
but now we buy the clothes we like.*

CHORUS

*We used to read by candlelight,
but now we use electric light.
We used to talk only face-to-face.
Now we use a mobile phone to talk
to someone in a different place.*

CHORUS

*People spent time with friends by the fire.
Now we play computer games instead.
But a friend is still a friend until the end.
Some things will never change!*

CHORUS

5 Work with a friend. Ask and answer.

1. How do you get to school? How did your parents get to school?

2. What do you do at the weekend? What did your parents do at the weekend when they were your age?

Luang Prabang, Laos

A long time ago, children walked to school, **but** I ride my bike.
Many years ago, people didn't have TV. They told stories **instead**.

6 Complete the sentences.

1. A long time ago, mothers and daughters sewed clothes at home.

   Today we buy clothes in shops _____.

2. Many years ago, people couldn't play computer games,

   _____ they had fun playing board games.

3. A long time ago, people didn't have computers.

   They wrote letters _____.

4. Many years ago, people didn't have cars, _____
   they had horses and carts.

Siberia, Russia

7 **Same or different?** Write true sentences.

A long time ago	Today
People had fireplaces.	We've got fireplaces, too.
People made their own soap.	We buy soap in a shop instead.
People walked everywhere.	
People played board games.	
People read by candlelight.	
People sewed their own clothes.	

8 **Work in a group.** Talk about your grandparents' lives and your life. How are they different?

My grandmother washed clothes by hand, but I use a washing machine instead!

9 **Listen and say.** Then read. Tick **T** for *True* or **F** for *False*. TR: A21

difficult

expensive

old-fashioned

important

modern

1. Computer games are modern toys.   Ⓣ Ⓕ

2. Parents say that cleaning your room is important.   Ⓣ Ⓕ

3. A rubber is expensive.   Ⓣ Ⓕ

4. Typewriters are old-fashioned.   Ⓣ Ⓕ

5. This sentence isn't difficult.   Ⓣ Ⓕ

10 **Work with a friend.** Talk and stick.

Look at this. What do you think?

It's very expensive.

1   2   3   4   5

Life was **more difficult** then.
That mobile phone is **more expensive than** this one.

11 Complete the sentences.

1. I think riding a skateboard is _____ (difficult) riding a bike.

2. Doing exercise is _____ (important) watching TV all day.

3. Computer games are _____ (expensive) board games.

4. Board games are _____ (old-fashioned) computer games, but they're fun to play.

5. Our new house is _____ (modern) our old one.

12 Play a game. Cut out the game board on page 163. Play with a friend. Make sentences about the pictures.

This phone is more old-fashioned than this one.

Heads: Move 1 space.

Tails: Move 2 spaces.

My turn!

From Walking to Biking

The bicycle is not the idea of just one person. Over time, many people contributed to its development.

The first bicycle was made of wood. It had two wheels but no pedals. You didn't ride it – you walked it! It was called a 'hobby horse' or 'walking machine'.

The velocipede came next. Velocipedes had pedals. Pedals were a good idea. With pedals, people could ride instead of walk or push their velocipedes. But velocipedes were hard to ride on cobblestone streets, and so they were called 'boneshakers'.

Later, people rode a new kind of bicycle called a 'penny-farthing'. It was made of metal and had a high front wheel and solid rubber tyres. It was more comfortable than a boneshaker, but people could fall off easily. Women didn't ride penny-farthings because women at the time wore long skirts. They rode a machine with three wheels, called a tricycle.

The next bicycle went back to two wheels of the same size. It had metal parts and pneumatic tyres, and was called the 'safety bicycle'. This design became the standard for modern bicycles. Then companies began to make bicycles for children. Now everyone enjoys bicycles!

Hobby Horse

Boneshaker

Penny-farthing

Tricycle

Safety Bicycle

seat

tyre

pedal

handlebars

wheel

14 Complete the sentences.

1. The hobby horse had two wheels but _____ pedals.

2. Velocipedes were _____ to ride on cobblestones.

3. Penny-farthings had _____ parts and rubber tyres.

4. Safety bikes had two wheels of the _____ size.

15 Complete the timeline. Read the text again.
Put the bicycles in order to complete the timeline.

| Boneshaker | Hobby Horse | Penny-farthing | Safety Bicycle | Tricycle |

1817   1870   1885

1863   1880

16 Work with a friend. Talk about bicycles. Ask and answer.

1. Are bicycles now just for children or for adults, too?
2. Have you got a bicycle? When and how do you use it?
3. Why are bicycles a good idea?

I ride my bike to school every day.

Weird but true

The longest bicycle ever made was about 36 metres (117 feet) long!

Paragraph Unity

In a paragraph, the topic sentence gives the main idea. The other sentences that make up the body give facts and examples about the main idea. A paragraph has unity when all the sentences refer to the main idea.

17 **Read.** This paragraph has five sentences that do not belong. Two are crossed out. Find the other three and cross them out.

School in the old days

A long time ago, school was different from the way it is now. Many towns had one-room schools, and all students were taught in the same one room. There was just one teacher, who taught all students of different ages. ~~All the students in my class are nine or ten years old.~~ Students sat on hard wooden benches in rows. ~~My class has got comfortable desks, one for each student.~~ They copied the alphabet, numbers and poems onto slates with chalk. They also practised their handwriting every day. They used quill pens and ink to write neatly. I use a computer to write. They copied texts and memorised long paragraphs from the one or two books the teacher had. I don't like memorising things from books. When students didn't do their work, the teacher used branches from trees to punish them. My teacher is kind, so she doesn't use branches. Some teachers made bad students stand in a corner and wear a pointed hat called a dunce's cap. Students felt ashamed and they looked silly, too. School is very different now.

18 **Write.** Write about life long ago. What did children do after school? What kinds of work did they do? What were their houses like? What clothes did children wear? Choose a topic. Make sure your paragraph has unity.

19 **Work in a group.** Share your writing. Listen and make notes.

NATIONAL GEOGRAPHIC

Mission
Appreciate the past.

'*The past is a source of knowledge and the future is a source of hope. Love of the past implies faith in the future.*'

Stephen Ambrose (1936–2002)
Historian
Explorer-in-Residence Emeritus

- Why is it important to appreciate the past? Discuss.

- What can you and other young people do to show how you appreciate the past? Work in a small group. Think of ideas. Discuss and write the best ideas in the box.

We can talk to our grandparents about their lives.

- Work with another group. Share your ideas. Are they the same or different? Which idea does everyone like best?

20 **Make a poster about life in the past and life now.**

1. Choose a topic such as clothing, toys, sport, food, houses or games.

2. Research information about your topic in the past and now.

3. Compare and contrast details related to your topic.

4. Cut out or draw pictures to support your writing.

5. Create a poster with your pictures and information.

6. Sign your poster.

Kites are my favourite toy. But they weren't always toys!

Now I can ...

○ describe what people did in the past.

○ talk about what the past was like.

○ compare the past and the present.

○ write a unified paragraph.

KITES

Kites are very old. People in China made kites 2,300 years ago. Then, kites weren't toys. They were military kites. They helped win wars. Some kites were big and strong. They carried soldiers!

Now we play with kites instead. They are more popular as works of art and as toys. There are beautiful kites for grown ups and fun kites for children.

THEN and NOW

Carlos

Review

1 **Listen.** How did this family live? Listen and draw lines from column A to B. TR: A24

A	B	C
We	sewed clothes	often.
My dad	washed the clothes	every day.
My mum and my sisters	began the day at 5 a.m.	twice a day.
My grandma	made the fire	sometimes.
I	told funny stories	at the weekend.
My grandpa	grew vegetables	once a week.

2 **Listen again.** How often did the family members do each activity? Draw lines from column B to C. TR: A25

3 **Work with a friend.** Compare life in that family and your life today. How is it different?

How is life different in your family?

We do, too. But on Saturday and Sunday we get up much later!

That family began the day at 5 a.m., but in my family we get up at 6 a.m.

4 **Work in groups of three.** Take turns. Ask and answer questions. Make notes.

1. How many brothers and sisters have you got?
2. Would you like another brother or sister?
3. Who is your favourite relative? Why?
4. Have most people in your family got straight, curly or wavy hair?
5. Who wears glasses in your family?
6. What is your family doing next weekend?

5 **Work in groups of three.** Compare your information.

I'd like a baby sister.

Me, too!

No way! I don't want a baby sister or brother!

6 **Look and read.** Read the sentences. Circle which clock each sentence is about.

a
£14.50

b
£19.90

c
£40.00

d
£45.00

1. This clock is for younger children. It's smaller than the other clock for children. **(a) b c d**
2. It is more modern than the other adult clock. **a b c d**
3. This one is good for children. It's more expensive than the other children's clock. **a b c d**
4. It is more old-fashioned than the other clocks. It's taller, too. **a b c d**
5. It is very nice. It's cheaper than the red clock. **a b c d**

7 **Write.** Compare two of the clocks. Use five words from the box.

| big | nice | expensive | funny | interesting |
| modern | old | old-fashioned | small | ugly |

My mum would like one of these clocks for her birthday. In some ways I think she'd like clock c more than clock d because . . .

Let's Talk

Hello!

I will …
- greet people (formally and informally).
- say thank you (formally and informally).

1 **Listen and read.** TR: A26

Sophie:	**Hello**, Mrs Green. **How are you?**
Mrs Green:	**I'm very well, thank you**, Sophie. Please come in.
Sophie:	Thank you.
Sophie:	**Hi**, Carla! **What's up?**
Carla:	**Not much.** Would you like a fizzy drink?
Sophie:	OK! **Thanks.**

Hello. Good morning. Good afternoon. Good evening.	**How are you?** How are you today?	**I'm very well, thank you.** I'm fine, **thanks**.
Hi! Hi there! Hey!	**What's up?** What are you doing? How're you doing? How's it going?	**Not much.** Nothing. Fine. I'm OK. Not bad.

2 **Work with a friend.** Greet each other. Use the table. Take turns.

I agree!

I will …
- ask for other people's opinions.
- agree and disagree.
- make generalisations.

3 **Listen and read.** TR: A27

Cho:	**What do you think about** making a poster?
Jong:	I think that's a great idea.
Mun-Hee:	**I agree.** Posters are fun.
Jin:	Really? **I disagree. Everybody makes posters!**
Hyo:	**I think so, too.**

What do you think (about) _____?	I agree. I agree with (Jong). Great idea!	I think so, too.
	I disagree.	Everybody makes _____.
Let's do a (report). What do you think?	Not again! Let's do something else.	(Surveys) are fun.
	Really? I don't think so.	(Reports) are boring.

4 **Listen.** You will hear two discussions. Read each question and circle the answer. TR: A28

1. How many students want to do a survey?
   a. 1   b. 2   c. 3

2. How many students want to write a report?
   a. 1   b. 2   c. 3

5 **Work in groups of four.** Prepare and practise discussions. Share your opinions about one of these projects.

- Preparing a talk about dinosaurs
- Making a poster about vegetables
- Doing a survey about housework

Unit 4

Get Well Soon!

In this unit, I will …
- talk about health and illness.
- describe actions.
- give advice.
- talk about cause and effect.

Look and answer.

1. What's the matter with her?
   She's got _____.

   ○ a cold

   ○ a broken arm

   ○ a headache

2. How do you think she feels?

   ○ It hurts a lot.

   ○ It hurts, but she feels fine.

   ○ Better than ever.

3. Write a speech bubble for this girl.

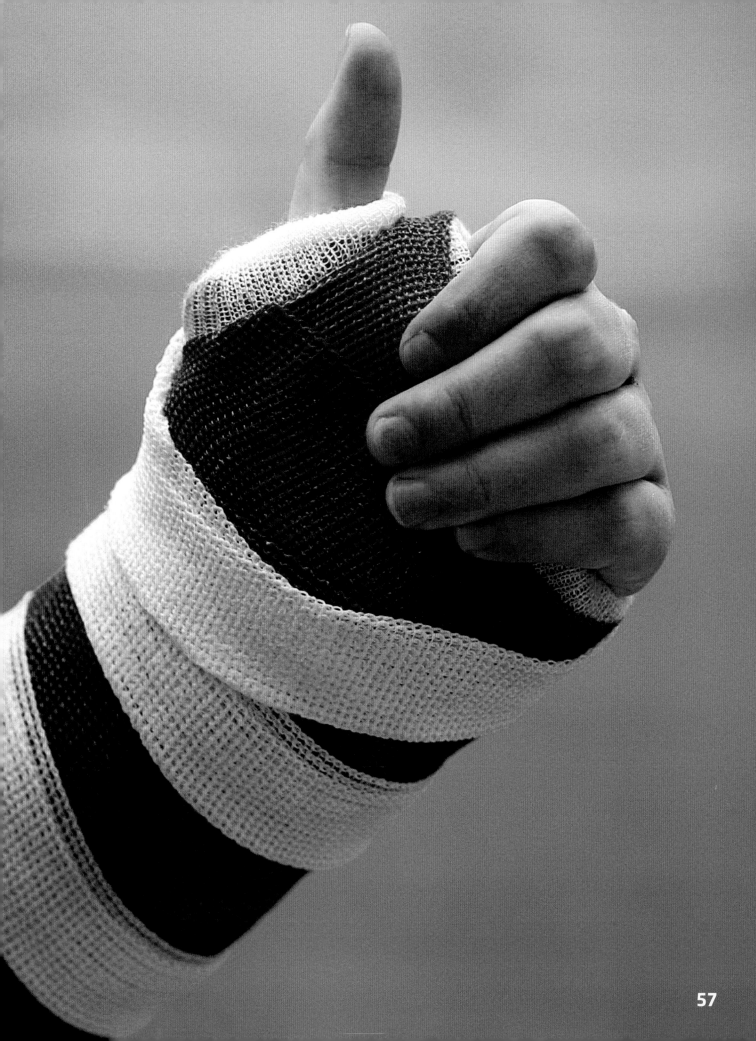

Our bodies are amazing. Every day they work hard to keep us healthy. But everyone gets ill sometimes. When you've got **a cold**, it means **germs** have entered your body. You can't see germs, but they can make you ill. Some germs can live for two hours on your desk. So use **tissues** when you **sneeze** or **cough**! And wash your hands with soap.

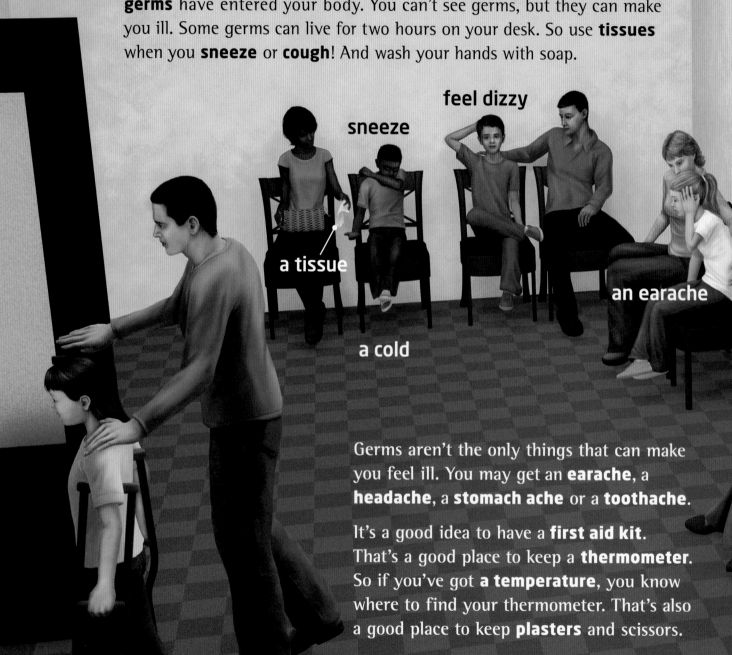

feel dizzy

sneeze

a tissue

a cold

an earache

a cast

Germs aren't the only things that can make you feel ill. You may get an **earache**, a **headache**, a **stomach ache** or a **toothache**.

It's a good idea to have a **first aid kit**. That's a good place to keep a **thermometer**. So if you've got **a temperature**, you know where to find your thermometer. That's also a good place to keep **plasters** and scissors.

Cover Your Mouth When You SNEEZE!

a germ

a thermometer

cough

a temperature

a toothache

a headache

a plaster

medicine

a bandage

a first aid kit

a stomach ache

3 **Work with a friend.** What did you learn? Ask and answer.

What's the matter with him?

He's got a stomach ache.

4 **Listen, read and sing.** TR: A31

Get Well Soon

Look after yourself. You know what to do.
Do a lot of exercise and eat the right food.
But once in a while, when you don't feel well,
here are some things that you should do.

If you've got a stomach ache
you should tell your mother.
If you've got a broken arm,
you should see the doctor.
If you've got a toothache,
you shouldn't eat sweets.
Go to the dentist and stay away
from treats.

CHORUS

If you scratch yourself when climbing a tree,
a first aid kit will help you to take care
of your knee.
If you've got a headache, you can stay in bed
or you can take some medicine
to help your aching head.

Look after yourself. You know what to do.
Do a lot of exercise and eat the right food.
But once in a while, when you don't feel well,
take very good care of yourself and get well soon!

5 **Work with a friend.** Write the problems and the solutions.

Problems	Solutions
stomach ache	tell your mother

I've got a bad toothache.   What **should** I do?
You **shouldn't** wait any longer.   Your mum **should** take you to the dentist.

6   **Read.** Complete the sentences.

1. If you've got a headache, you ___*shouldn't eat*___ (not / eat) any more ice cream.

2. Everybody _____ (have) a first aid kit at home.

3. He's got a temperature. He _____ (not / go) to school.

4. She feels dizzy. She _____ (sit) down.

5. When you've got a cold, you _____ (not / sneeze) on people.

6. You _____ (use) tissues.

7. What _____ you _____ (do) when you've got a toothache?

8. You _____ (exercise) two or three times a week.

7 **Read and write.** Write some advice for this family.

Stay at home.
Don't go to school.

Go to the dentist.
Don't eat sweets.

Cover your mouth.
Don't cough on other people.

Lie down.
Don't drive your car.

1. <u>The boy has got a temperature. He should stay at home. He shouldn't go to school.</u>

2. _____

3. _____

4. _____

8 **Work in a group.** Act out an illness. Guess and give advice.
Take turns.

Atishoo!!

You've got a cold. You shouldn't sneeze near me!

Ugh! You should use some tissues!

9 **Listen and repeat.** Read and circle the letter. TR: A33

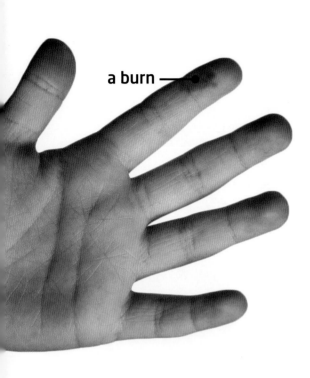

a burn

a broken leg

a scratch

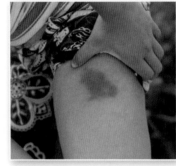

a bruise

a cut

1. Why is your leg in a cast?   a. I've got a broken leg.   b. I've got a bruise.

2. Is that a burn?   a. Yes, I've got a headache.   b. Yes, I touched the cooker!

3. I've got a scratch. What should I do?

  a. You should put a plaster on it.   b. You should go to the dentist.

4. What an ugly bruise. What happened to her?

  a. She had a bike accident.   b. She ate too much chocolate.

5. How did you get that cut?

  a. I ran with scissors.   b. I ate too much ice cream.

10 **Work with a friend.** Listen. Talk and stick. TR: A34

What happened on Monday?

Her brother got a cut on his finger.

Monday	Tuesday	Wednesday	Thursday	Friday

Ouch! I cut **myself**.
Be careful. Don't hurt **yourself**.
My brother burnt **himself** on the cooker. He shouldn't cook by **himself**.
Look at that bandage. Did she hurt **herself**?

a cut ⟶ to cut
a burn ⟶ to burn

11 **Read and write.** Complete the sentences.

1. Last week I ran with scissors and I fell. I cut _____.

2. When my sister touched the cooker, she burnt

_____. It was terrible.

3. If you scratch _____, you should put on a plaster.

4. My brother didn't listen to me, and he hurt _____.

12 **Play a game.** Cut out the cards on page 165.
Glue the cards. Listen. TR: A36

1	2	3
4		5
6	7	8

Why Do We Sneeze?

Atishoo! When you've got a cold, you often sneeze. Why? Because germs make a home in your nose and they tickle you! Sneezing is your body's way of sending germs out of your nose. Many animals sneeze, too!

What happens? Your nose doesn't like the germs, so it sends a message to a part of your brain called the 'sneeze centre'. The sneeze centre sends a message to your muscles. Then, all your muscles push hard. Even your eyes push. That's why you close your eyes when you sneeze! You should have a tissue ready because the sneeze happens very quickly. A sneeze can travel as fast as a car!

Some people sneeze when they haven't got a cold. It happens when they go out into the sunshine. They are called 'photic sneezers'. Photic sneezing is an inherited trait. It comes from one of your parents. Do you know anyone who sneezes because of the sun?

A sneeze from one person on a train can reach 150 other people.

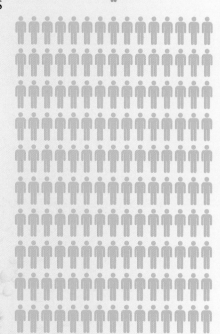

Iguanas sneeze more than any other animal!

germs

66

14 **Read.** Tick **T** for *True* or **F** for *False*.

1. Germs live in your nose all the time.   Ⓣ Ⓕ

2. The sneeze centre is in your brain.   Ⓣ Ⓕ

3. People always sneeze when they catch a cold.   Ⓣ Ⓕ

4. We get colds from our parents. They are inherited.   Ⓣ Ⓕ

15 **Read.** Read the text again. Put the sentences in order.

_____ Your nose tickles.

_____ The germs go out of your nose.

_____ Your nose sends a message to the sneeze centre in the brain.

_____ Your muscles push hard.

_____ Your brain tells your muscles to stop the tickle.

16 **Work with a friend.** Ask questions and make notes. Take turns.

How many people can a sneeze reach?

It can reach 150 people.

Sneezing	
Why?	
Who?	
How?	
How fast?	
How many people?	

Paragraphs of Cause and Effect

In a paragraph of cause and effect, you explain what happens and why. You use words like *because*, *that's why* and *that's because* to show cause and effect.

17 **Read.** Read the paragraph of cause and effect. How does the writer explain what happens and the reasons why? Circle the words and expressions.

Ice-cream headaches

Do you ever get a headache when you eat ice cream? Many people do. Why? Because your body doesn't like the cold temperature of the ice cream! Here's what happens. The ice cream is very cold. When the ice cream touches the roof of your mouth, the nerve centre doesn't like the cold. It sends a message to your brain. Then, the brain sends a message to your blood vessels, and they get big very quickly. That's because they are trying to keep your head warm.

So, that's why you get ice-cream headaches! But they aren't serious, so don't worry! They are easy to prevent, too. Just keep cold food and drink away from the roof of your mouth! You should eat cold food slowly, and put the ice cream in the front of your mouth first.

18 **Write.** Choose another common health problem. Write what happens and why. Use words and expressions to explain the reasons.

19 **Work in a group.** Share your writing. Listen and make notes.

NATIONAL GEOGRAPHIC

Mission

Be prepared.

'*My mission is to find simple, inexpensive ways to check on the health of people in distant places and difficult conditions.*'

Hayat Sindi, UNESCO Goodwill Ambassador for Sciences
Emerging Explorer

- How can we be prepared for illness and accidents? Work in a small group. Think of ideas. Discuss and write the best ideas in the box.

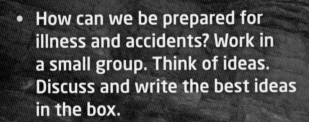

Keep a first aid kit at home.

_____

_____

_____

_____

- Work with another group. Share your ideas. Are they the same or different? Which ideas does everyone like best?

A rope rescue in Sedona, Arizona, USA

20 **Make a first aid kit for your family.**

1. Research what you need in a first aid kit.

   a. Find out about basic needs.
   b. Find out about special needs, such as medicine.

2. Make a list of what you need.

3. Make a kit.

   a. Find a lunchbox (or other strong box). Decorate it.
   b. Put all items and supplies in it.

4. Write down some important telephone numbers. Put them inside the box. Add the numbers to your mobile phone.

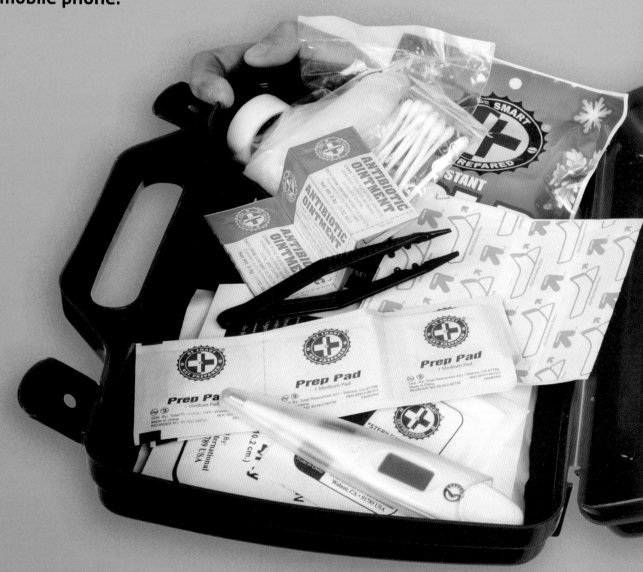

A first aid kit should have plasters.
I packed plasters for cuts.

FIRST AID KIT

Now I can ...

- ◯ talk about health and illness.
- ◯ describe actions.
- ◯ give advice.
- ◯ talk about cause and effect.

Unit 5
My Favourites

In this unit, I will …
- identify different types of entertainment.
- compare people and activities.
- talk about my favourite people and things.
- give my opinion.

Tick T for *True* or F for *False*.

1. Everyone looks happy. (T) (F)

2. Some people look scared. (T) (F)

3. They are riding on
   a roller coaster. (T) (F)

Genting, Pahang, Malaysia

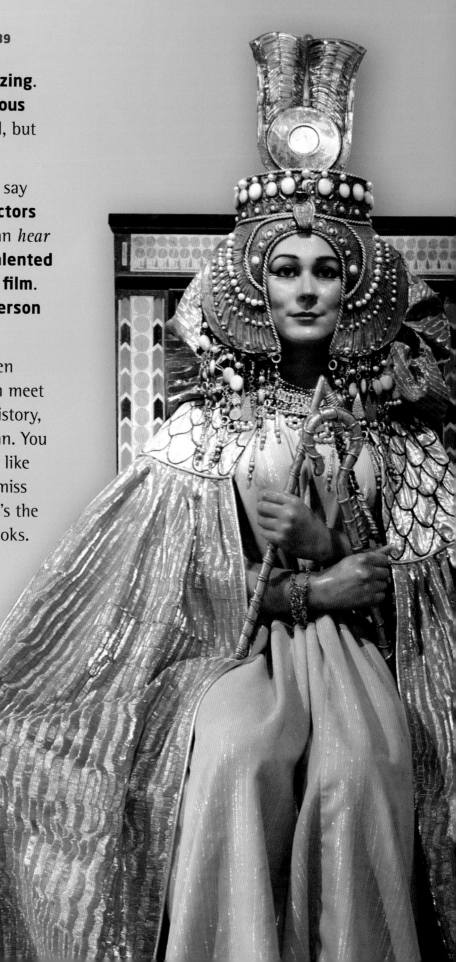

1 **Listen and read.** TR: A38

2 **Listen and repeat.** TR: A39

Waxworks museums are **amazing**. You can see hundreds of **famous** people. The people aren't real, but they look real!

In these **cool** places, you can say 'Hello' to all your favourite **actors** and **popular** TV stars. You can *hear* some of them, too! Meet a **talented** singer or actor from a **funny film**. Take photos with a famous **person** or a **brave** superhero!

There are many **pretty** women and **handsome** men. You can meet interesting characters from history, like Cleopatra or Genghis Khan. You can stand next to an **athlete** like Yao Ming. He's **great**. Don't miss J.K. Rowling's characters. She's the author of the Harry Potter books. They are **wonderful**!

Who would you like to see at a waxworks museum?

Cleopatra, Courtesy of the Wax Museum of Madrid

an athlete

3 **Work with a friend.** What did you learn?
Ask and answer.

Can you see athletes in the museum?

Yes, you can. Yao Ming is there!

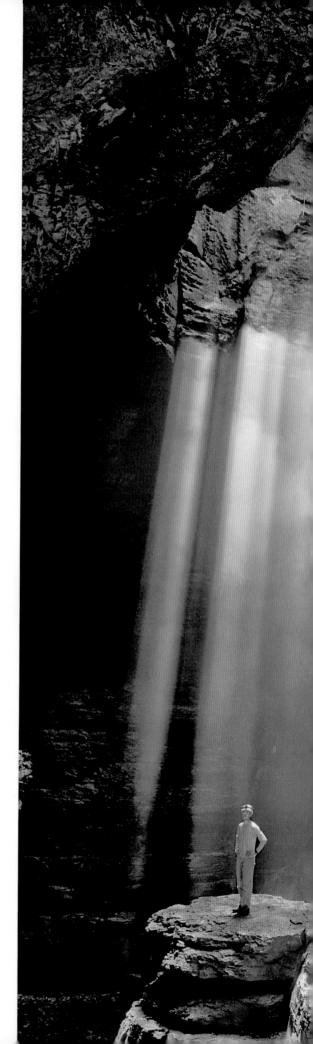

4 Listen, read and sing. TR: A40

You're the Best

How do I know what I'll want one day?
How do I know what I'll be?
Who can help me to find my way
and show me how to be a better me?

I really like playing football.
One day I could be great!
I'll learn from my favourite athletes:
work hard, practise and wait!

Someday I'll dream of fans and fame
in films and on TV.
I watch my favourite actors' films
I'll be just like them, you'll see!

CHORUS

I really love the natural world:
jungles, mountains and caves.
Like my favourite explorers,
I'll go on adventures for days and days!

I read the most talented writers,
dream about writing a book.
I'll work very hard in school.
Becoming a writer would be so good!

CHORUS

5 **Work with a friend.** Choose two professions from the song. Make a list of three interesting things about each profession. Then share your lists with a small group. Are they the same or different?

Stephens Gap Cave, Alabama

I think Yao Ming is **the greatest** basketball player in the world.
J.K. Rowling is **the most talented** writer I know.
In your opinion, what's **the funniest** film of all?

6 **Read.** Complete the questions.

1. Who is ___the most amazing singer___ in the world? (amazing / singer)

2. In your opinion, who is _____? (amazing / athlete)

3. In your opinion, what is _____? (pretty / flower)

4. What is _____ you watch? (interesting / TV show)

5. What is _____ of all? (funny / film)

6. In your opinion, who is _____? (talented / TV star)

7 **Look at the pictures.** Write sentences.

1. big

The red car is bigger than the green car, but the blue car is the biggest!

2. beautiful
 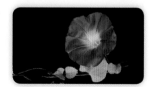 

_____

3. cool

_____

8 **What about you?** Work with a friend. Ask and answer.
Complete the table. Take turns.

Questions	Me	My partner
1. who / talented / singer		
2. who / cool / TV star		
3. what / interesting / computer game		
4. who / amazing / actor		
5. what / funny / film		
6. who / great / athlete		

9 **Work in a small group.** Compare your opinions.
Decide who or what is the group's favourite.

Who is the most talented singer?

Bocelli.

Who's he?

Are you joking? He's the greatest opera singer ever!

10 **Listen and repeat.** Then read and match. TR: A42

a TV show

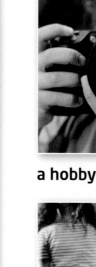

a hobby

a school subject

a sport   a writer

1. What's your favourite sport?

2. My parents watch a lot of boring TV shows!

3. Which country is that writer from?

4. What are your favourite hobbies?

5. What's your favourite school subject?

a. I like playing sports and going out with my friends.

b. Well, I like tennis. But I think football is the best.

c. I haven't got one. I like all my school subjects.

d. She's from India. She's very talented.

e. My parents do, too!

11 **Work with a friend.** Stick and talk. Take turns.

> I put sports first. I love football!

> I put sports last! I don't like them.

1   2   3   4   5

I'm **good** at music. I'm **better** than my friend at sports. And I'm **the best** in our class at English!

A cough is **bad**; a cold is **worse**; but a stomach ache is **the worst**!

12 **Complete the sentences.**

1. Many computer games are _____ because they're boring.

   But 'Harry Potter, the Goblet of Fire', is _____ than other

   games because it's more interesting. You can be Harry, Ron or Hermione

   in the computer game. Harry is _____ person to be in

   the game because he's intelligent and he helps other people. Ron is

   _____ person to be because he isn't funny.

2. I love football. It is _____ spare-time activity of all! It's

   much _____ than TV because you go out and have fun.

   I think TV is _____ for your health because you don't

   do any exercise. And computer games are _____ than

   TV because you don't learn anything!

13 **Play a game.** Cut out
the cards on page 167.
Play with a friend.

What's the best computer game?

The new Harry Potter computer game is the best.

81

Amazing Acrobats

Many acts we see in circuses today have roots in ancient societies. Jugglers and acrobats were popular in ancient Egypt and China. Today, Chinese circuses are more popular, more colourful and more exciting than ever.

Most Chinese acrobats join the circus when they are six years old, but they can spend ten years practising just one of these acts!

a. Juggling: Acrobats use their feet to juggle things. They juggle tables, chairs, umbrellas, plates and even people!

b. Cycling: In this act, acrobats use 'monocycles' (bicycles with one wheel). The most famous act is the 'bird'.

c. Tightrope: This act is about 2,000 years old. Brave acrobats walk, cycle or jump on a wire that is high in the air.

d. Pole-climbing: This act is about 1,000 years old. Athletes climb up poles, jump from one pole to the other and balance on the poles.

e. Plate-spinning: The acrobat holds a pole with a plate on it. The plates spin fast. The acrobat dances, jumps or stands on one arm.

Don't miss Chinese acrobats. They're the best!

China

weird but true Some Chinese acrobats called 'gastriloquists' make the sound of birds, animals, crying babies and machines while they do their acts.

15 Read and write.

1. In what ancient societies were jugglers and acrobats popular?

_____

2. How old are many children when they start to learn acrobatics?

_____

3. How long do acrobats have to practise to learn some acts?

_____

4. What things do acrobats juggle?

_____

16 Read. Label the pictures *a-e*.

bird

17 Work in a group. Compare your opinions. Write your group's decision in each box.

Acrobat tricks			
Most difficult	Easiest	Most interesting	Group favourite

I think juggling is the most difficult.

No! Walking on a tightrope is much more difficult.

Reviews

When you write a review, you tell the reader about the story and give your opinions. Use words like *in my opinion*, *I think* and *I believe*. Use descriptive words like *interesting*, *exciting* and *boring*. When you give your opinions, you can give a reason, too.

18 **Read.** Read the book review. How does the writer express her opinion? Underline the words and expressions.

Last weekend I went to the library with my dad and I found a wonderful book by Jacqueline Wilson. It's called 'Cliffhanger'. I always look for her books. In my opinion, she is one of the best writers in the world.

'Cliffhanger' is about a boy called Tim. He likes TV shows and puzzles. He's very clever, too, and he's the best student at most school subjects. But he's the worst student at sports! So when his parents send him to a sports camp, he has a horrible time.

Every day at camp Tim has to do sport, and he never gets better. He hates sport. But one day he has a clever idea about how to win the game. After that, he helps his team win and he's the most popular person at camp. Then he doesn't want to leave!

I loved this book. Jacqueline Wilson helps us to remember some important things. Firstly, that we are all different. Secondly, you shouldn't feel sad if you are not handsome, because everyone is talented in some way. Finally, sometimes you are not popular. But you have to try!

19 **Write.** Write about something you liked, for example, a book you read or a film you watched. Tell the story and say why you liked it.

20 **Work in a group.** Share your writing. Listen and make notes.

Mission

Find a role model.

- Think about a person who inspires you. Why is he or she special?

- Do you want to be like this person? Why?

- Work in a small group. Describe your role models. Discuss what they do that inspires you. Which role models does everyone like best? Make notes.

'When I was a young girl, I always wanted to work with wildlife. But it's only because I had really great science teachers in school who gave me that interest in biology.'

Aparajita Datta
Wildlife Biologist
Emerging Explorer

My role models are sportspeople.

- Work with another group. Share your information. Which role models are the most interesting?

Bengal tiger, Bandhavgarh National Park, India

21 **Make a class book about famous people.**

1. Think about who your favourite famous person is.

   • What does he or she do? Why is he or she famous?
   • What do you like about him or her?

2. Research some information about your favourite person.

3. Make a page for the class book.

   • Glue a picture.
   • Write a summary about your favourite person.

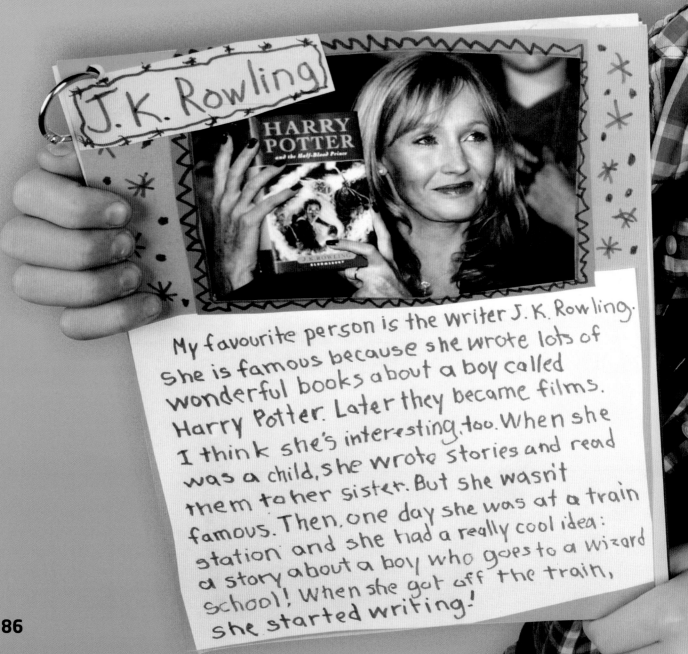

J.K. Rowling

HARRY POTTER

My favourite person is the writer J. K. Rowling. She is famous because she wrote lots of wonderful books about a boy called Harry Potter. Later they became films. I think she's interesting, too. When she was a child, she wrote stories and read them to her sister. But she wasn't famous. Then, one day she was at a train station and she had a really cool idea: a story about a boy who goes to a wizard school! When she got off the train, she started writing!

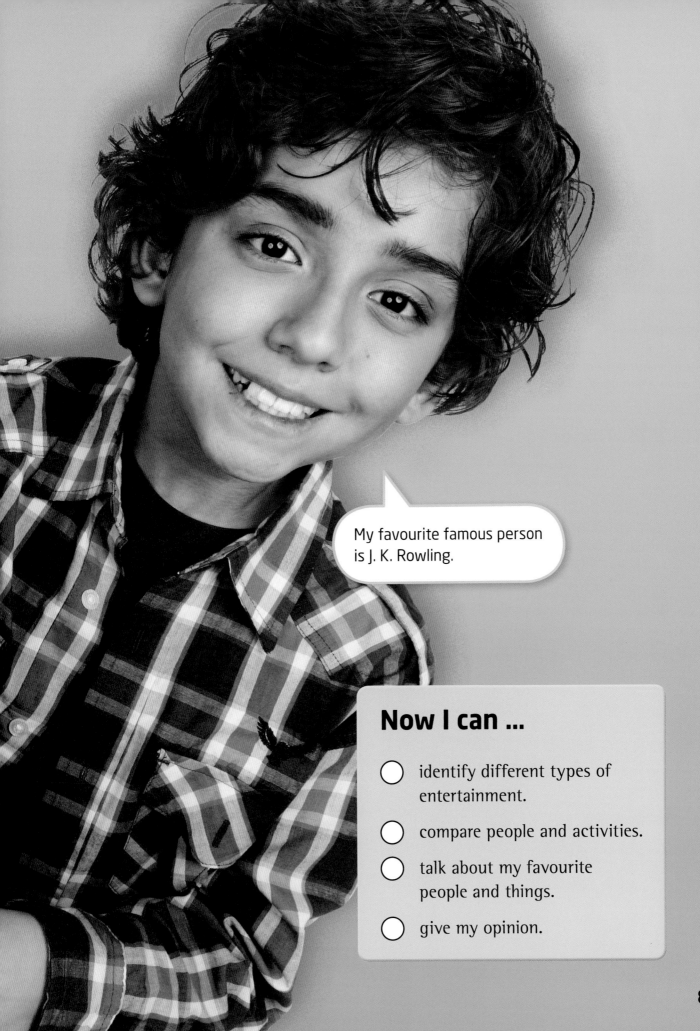

My favourite famous person is J. K. Rowling.

Now I can ...

○ identify different types of entertainment.

○ compare people and activities.

○ talk about my favourite people and things.

○ give my opinion.

Unit 6

Wonders
of the Sea

In this unit, I will …
- identify sea life.
- describe characteristics of sea life.
- talk about protecting the sea.
- write a paragraph of contrast.

Tick T for *True* or F for *False*.

1. There are lots of animals
   in the picture. **T** **F**

2. This is an octopus. **T** **F**

3. An octopus's got six arms. **T** **F**

4. An octopus can change colour. **T** **F**

Blue-ringed octopus

1 **Listen and read.** TR: B2

2 **Listen and repeat.** TR: B3

We use the sea for fun, for transport and, more importantly, we use the sea for food. We must stop **pollution**. We must protect the sea or our **resources** will **disappear**.

The sea is full of wonderful sea life. Most of the **creatures** we know stay near the top **layer** of the water, called the **sunlight zone**. In this zone, **sunlight** goes down to about 137 metres (450 feet).

a whale

The middle layer of the water is called the twilight zone. This is because there isn't much light. This zone goes down to about 1,000 metres (3,300 feet). Few creatures live in this layer.

a squid

The mysterious bottom layer of water is completely black. It is called the **midnight** zone because sunlight doesn't reach below 1,000 metres (3,300 feet). Some amazing animals live in this deepest part of the sea.

a fish

a dolphin

a turtle

a shark

sea sponges

an octopus

3 **Work with a friend.** What did you learn? Ask and answer.

Where do squid live?

In the twilight zone.

4 Listen, read and sing. TR: B4

Protect the Sea

Please, please protect the sea.
Do what's good for you and me
and help us save the sea.

CHORUS

We must protect
the wonders of the sea,
to make a better world
for you and me.

We must stop polluting
the sea so blue.
An octopus would like that
and so would you.

CHORUS

We must protect
the wonders of the sea,
to make a better world
for you and me.

Please remember,
don't throw rubbish into the sea.
Sharks wouldn't want that.
Would we?

There are layers in the sea below.
There are creatures there that we don't know.
They live deep underwater. They don't breathe air,
but our world is a part of theirs.

CHORUS

5 Work with a friend.

Ask and answer.

1. What are two common ways we pollute the sea?

2. What are some ways we use the sea?

3. Why is it important to care for the sea?

Humpback whale, Alaska, USA

We **have to** keep the sea clean.　　You **can't** throw rubbish into the sea.
We **must** protect the sea.　　**Don't** leave food on the beach.

6 **Tick.** Right or wrong?

	Right	Wrong
1. We must throw plastic bags in the sea.		✓
2. Don't leave rubbish in the classroom.		
3. You have to throw rubbish in the rivers.		
4. You can't use biodegradable things. They will never disappear.		
5. We must protect natural habitats.		

7 **Read.** Complete the sentences.

1. _____We must_____ protect the whales and the dolphins.

2. _____ throw bottles into the sea.

3. _____ respect and protect nature.

4. _____ help with the housework.

5. _____ leave rubbish in the classroom.

8 **What about you?** Write about rules at home and at school.

At home, _I have to tidy my room every day._

_____

_____

_____

_____

At school, _____

_____

_____

_____

9 **Work in a group.** Compare your rules.

At school, don't leave rubbish in the classroom.

At home, we have to help our parents to clean up.

95

10 **Listen and repeat.** Then read and write. TR: B6

an oil spill

rubbish

overfishing

plastic bags

not **biodegradable**

a paper bag

biodegradable

1. Banana skins, plastic bottles, fizzy drinks cans, old newspapers, boxes and broken toys

   are examples of __rubbish_____.

2. When companies catch too many fish all the time, there aren't enough

   fish left to reproduce. This is called _____.

3. Paper is _____. With time, it disappears.

4. Bottles and bags made out of _____ are not biodegradable.

5. Big ships called tankers transport oil across the sea. When they have an

   accident and oil escapes, the result is an _____.

11 **Work with a friend.** Listen, talk and stick. TR: B7

Oil spills happen when tankers have accidents on the sea.

That's right.

1 2 3 4 5

What **will** happen in the future?   Sea animals and plants **will** disappear.
We **won't** have as much food as we need.

12 **Read and answer.**

1. Oil pollution affects the sunlight zone of the sea.
   What if there is a big oil spill?

   _____

2. Pollution affects oxygen levels in the midnight zone and creates
   areas with no oxygen. What if there are animals in these areas?

   _____

3. Plastic bottles and plastic bags cause a lot of pollution.
   What will you do?

   _____

   _____

13 **Play a game.** Cut out seven pictures and the bingo card
on page 169. Listen and play. Discuss. TR: B9

Colourful Corals

When you first see corals, you may think you are looking at a colourful underwater garden. But corals are animals, not plants. Corals are made up of small individual animals called polyps. Polyps have soft, transparent bodies with no bones inside.

What's for dinner? Polyps have a mouth, stomach and tentacles to catch food. How polyps get food depends on where they live. Polyps lucky enough to live in warm, sunlight zones eat tiny plants called algae. In contrast, polyps that live in cold, dark zones don't eat algae. They must find a place to live with a strong current of moving water. They use their tentacles to catch tiny animals called plankton in the water.

Underwater communities. Most corals live together in huge groups called colonies. Some build a protective skeleton around themselves. As old generations die and new ones grow on top, polyps slowly build up coral reefs. Some are millions of years old. These beautiful reefs are home to more than 4,000 kinds of fish and thousands of other organisms.

Save the reefs! Coral reefs are a source of food for many communities. They are also a source of tourism and jobs for local people. Scientists use reef animals to develop new medicines and other products. But coral reefs are in danger. Because of pollution, many coral reefs will disappear. Some experts predict that only 30 per cent of the world's corals will exist in the year 2050. We must protect our corals now.

The Great Barrier Reef is over 2,250 kilometers (1,400 miles) long! You can see it from outer space!

15 **Read.** Complete the definitions.

1. Corals are made up of individual animals called _____.

2. Warm-water polyps eat tiny plants called _____.

3. Cool-water polyps eat tiny animals called _____.

4. Most corals live in very large groups called _____.

16 **Label.** Look and read the text again. Then write a label for each number.

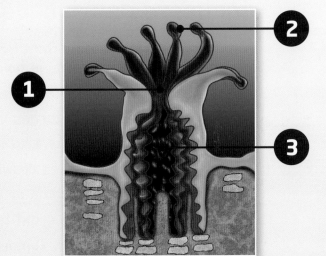

1. _____

2. _____

3. _____

17 **Work with a friend.** Choose warm or cool corals to talk about. Your friend will listen and complete the first column. Then listen to your friend and fill in the second column.

Type of coral		
They are made up of		
They live in		
They eat		

Paragraphs of Contrast

In a paragraph of contrast, you write about the differences between two things. You can use facts and descriptive words to show differences. You can also use words that show contrast, such as *but* and *however*, and expressions such as *in contrast*.

18 **Read.** Read about tortoises and turtles. How does the writer show differences? Underline the words and expressions.

Tortoises and turtles

Tortoises and turtles begin their lives on land. The mothers lay their eggs in holes and then cover them up to protect the eggs. But after that, baby tortoises' and turtles' lives are very different. Depending on the kind of tortoise they are, the baby tortoises crawl away to live in woods, swamps, grasslands or deserts. In contrast, the baby turtles crawl to the sea to live their lives in the water. Tortoises and turtles look different, too. A tortoise's shell is hard, high and round. When they are afraid, they hide in their shells. However, a turtle's shell is softer and flatter. They can't hide inside, but they can swim away really quickly. When cold weather comes, tortoises dig holes in the ground and sleep all winter. They are too slow to move to warmer places. In contrast, turtles simply swim away to find warmer waters.

tortoise

turtle

19 **Write.** Write about warm and cool corals. How are they different? Use words and expressions that show contrast.

20 **Work in a group.** Share your writing.

NATIONAL GEOGRAPHIC

Mission

Protect the sea.

- Why must we protect the sea? Discuss.

- Work in a small group. What can you do to help? Discuss your ideas and write the best ideas in the box.

'With every drop of water you drink, every breath you take, you're connected to the ocean. No matter where on Earth you live. Taking care of the ocean means taking care of us.'

Sylvia Earle, Oceanographer
Explorer-in-Residence

I can take part in a beach clean-up.

_____

_____

_____

_____

- Get together with another group. Share your ideas. Are they the same or different? Which idea does everyone like best?

Sylvia Earle diving, Honduras

21 **Make posters and cards about ways to help sea animals.**

1. Research information.

2. Make posters.

3. Make cards to hand out.

4. Invite people to a community clean-up.

5. At your event, take photos for a school newspaper article.

Our poster is about why it's important to protect coral reefs.

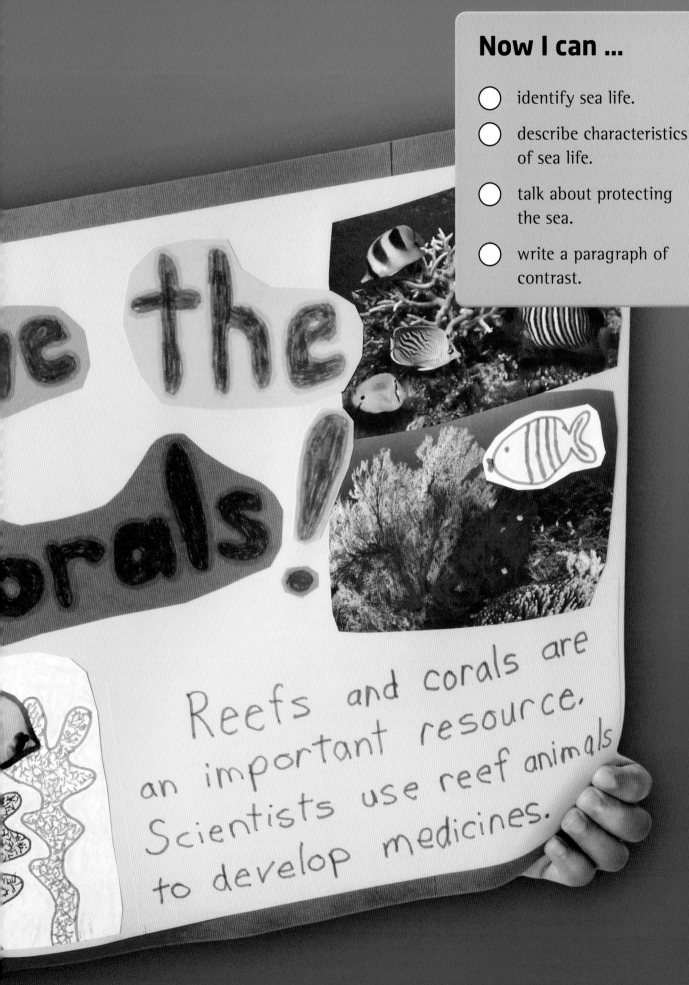

Reefs and corals are an important resource. Scientists use reef animals to develop medicines.

Now I can ...

○ identify sea life.

○ describe characteristics of sea life.

○ talk about protecting the sea.

○ write a paragraph of contrast.

Review

1 **Listen.** Weiwei is doing a survey. Write her questions in the table. TR: B11

Topic	Question	Jun	Ming
Creature	1.	octopus	
Writer	2.		Bruce Coville
Athlete	3.	Usain Bolt	
School	4.		English
Illness	5.	a broken arm	

2 **Listen again.** Write Jun and Ming's answers in the table. TR: B12

3 **Write.** Prepare five questions like Weiwei's for your classmates.

handsome	interesting	actor	TV show
popular	funny	person	film
pretty	great	hobby	relative
wonderful	best / worst	sport	singer

4 **Work in a group of three.** Take turns. Ask and answer the questions you wrote. Do you have any favourite things in common?

5 **Look and read.** Look at the pictures below. What's wrong?
Match the sentences.

1. The cooker is still hot.

2. The milk bottle is near the window.

3. The girl is wearing a cast.

4. The medicine bottle is open.

a. Adults should always put medicine away.

b. If the cat touches it, it will fall.

c. He must not touch it or he'll burn himself.

d. She shouldn't climb a tree.

6 **Look and write.** Look at the pictures again. What else is wrong?

1. The boy is running with scissors. He _____ with scissors.

2. The man isn't wearing his hat. He _____ a hat in the sun.

3. The girl wants to touch the knife. She _____ it.

7 **Work with a friend.** Ask and answer.

1. Why shouldn't you sneeze on people? What should you do instead?

2. You feel dizzy. Is it better to lie down or do some exercise?

3. Why shouldn't we throw plastic into the sea?

8 **Work with another friend.** Compare your answers.
Are they the same or different?

Let's Talk

What's wrong?

I will …
• ask how someone is feeling.
• describe how I feel.
• show that I care or understand.
• make a suggestion.

1 Listen and read. TR: B13

Aziz: **What's wrong?**

Sawsan: **I feel sick.**

Aziz: **Oh, no.** What's the problem?

Sawsan: I've got a stomach ache.

Aziz: **Why don't you** tell Mum?

Sawsan: Yes, that's a good idea. Mum!

What's wrong?	**I feel sick.**	**Oh, no.**	**Why don't you**
What's up?	I don't feel well.	I'm sorry.	_____?
What's the problem?	I'm not feeling well.	Oh, I'm really sorry.	You should _____.
What's the matter?	I'm tired.	That's a shame.	Maybe you should
	I'm hungry.		_____.
	I'm cross with my brother.		

2 Work with a friend. Describe how you feel. Use the table.
Take turns.

I don't understand.

I will …
• politely interrupt.
• express confusion.
• check that someone understands.
• thank someone and reply.

3 **Listen and read.** TR: B14

Nikolai: Let's start the game.

Olga: **Hang on! I'm lost.** How do we play?

Nikolai: First, you have to spin the spinner.
Then you move your counter. **Got it?**

Olga: Yes, **I think so. Thanks.**

Nikolai: **No problem.**

Hang on!	I'm lost.	Got it?	I think so. Thanks.	No problem.
Wait a moment, please. Wait. Wait a minute. Hold on.	I don't understand. I don't get it.	Does that make sense? Does that help? OK?	Oh, I see! Thanks. Oh, I get it now. Thanks.	You're welcome. That's OK. It's a pleasure.

4 **Listen.** You will hear two discussions. Read each question and circle the answer. TR: B15

1. Does the boy understand the instructions after the girl explains them?
   a. yes   b. no

2. Which expression does the boy use?
   a. Do you see now?   b. Got it?   c. OK?

5 **Work in pairs.** Practise discussions. Imagine you are playing one of these games. One student doesn't understand. The other explains.

1. Noughts and crosses
2. Bingo
3. Rock, paper, scissors

Unit 7

Good Idea!

In this unit, I will ...
- talk about inventions.
- talk about habits in the past.
- describe how to use an invention.
- write about facts and opinions.

Look and tick.

This is a

- ⚪ rocket.
- ⚪ aeroplane.
- ⚪ train.

A high-speed bullet train, Tokyo, Japan

1 **Listen and read.** TR: B16

2 **Listen and repeat.** TR: B17

Inventions are everywhere. Look around you. What inventions can you see?

Five thousand years ago people had a **problem**. They couldn't move things! Then someone found the **solution** – the **wheel**. It changed our lives.

Imagine your life without **electricity**. Before electricity, we didn't have **useful** things such as **batteries**, computers and mobile phones.

electricity

a battery

a wheel

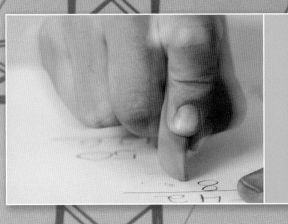

Inventors need **imagination** and **creativity**. Before the rubber, people used bread to rub out writing! In 1839 Charles Goodyear had an **idea**. He **invented** the modern rubber.

The Wright brothers **tried** to fly many times, but they **failed**. Finally they **succeeded** in 1903. Alberto Santos-Dumont also tried many times. He made the first public flight in the world. Now that we have aeroplanes, our world is very different.

3 **Work with a friend.** What did you learn? Ask and answer.

When did the Wright brothers fly an aeroplane?

They flew an aeroplane in 1903.

Listen, read and sing. TR: B18

Inventions

Creativity!
Electricity!
Creativity changes the world!

Inventions solve problems.
Problems that we used to have are gone!
The wheel and the mobile phone
help to make our world go round!

Inventions are useful,
every day, in every way.
Computers, cars and aeroplanes
help to make our world go round!

CHORUS

You used to have to walk
to get from place to place.
Years ago, you could only talk
face-to-face.
You could only get across the sea by boat.
Now we fly across the sky.
Inventions are the reason why.

CHORUS

Imagination and ideas
can change the world, every day.
Can you solve a problem?
Can you help our world today?

CHORUS

5 **Work with a friend.** Discuss.

1. What inventions are mentioned in the song?

2. Which invention do you think is the most important? Why?

People **used to** rub out writing with bread.

We **didn't use to** have rubbers.

Why **did** people **use to** read by candlelight?

They **didn't use to** have electricity.

6 **Read.** Complete the sentences. Tick the true sentences.

1. Before the invention of the rubber, people _used to rub out_

   (rub out) writing with water. _____

2. Before the invention of cars, people _____

   _____ (ride) horses in the city. _____

3. Before the invention of the aeroplane, people _____

   _____ (not / travel) by air. _____

4. In the 1950s, people _____

   (not / make) calls with a mobile phone. _____

5. We _____ (not / have)

   computers before there was electricity. _____

7 **Work with a friend.** Ask and answer.

1. What did people use to do for fun before TV?

2. How did people use to travel before aeroplanes?

3. What did children use to play with before computer games?

8 **What about you?** Write five sentences about when you were younger. Write two that *aren't* true. Use these words to help you.

toys	games	brothers and sisters	TV shows	music
home	holidays	spare-time activities	clothes	hair colour

1. _____

_____

2. _____

_____

3. _____

_____

4. _____

_____

5. _____

_____

9 **Work with a friend.** Read your sentences. Take turns.

When I was six, I used to ride my bike to school.

That's not true! Your dad used to drive you to school. I saw you!

115

10 **Listen and repeat.** TR: B20
Complete. Then listen and
check your answers. TR: B21

waist

turn

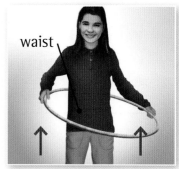

lift

put
hoop

move

use

The 'hula hoop' is an old invention, but it's very popular today.
It's fun and it's good exercise!

1. How do you ___use___ a hula hoop? It's easy.
   Follow these instructions.

2. _____ the hula hoop on the ground. Stand in the middle.

3. _____ the hoop to your waist.

4. _____ your waist in a circle. Don't hold the hoop!

5. The hoop _____ round and round. Can you feel it?

11 **Listen and stick.** Put the stickers in order. Then tell your friend
how to use this toy. Use the stickers to help you remember! TR: B22

| 1 | 2 | 3 | 4 | 5 |

You need to have creativity to invent things.

You should always try again if **you** fail.

What do **you** do with this invention?

Do **you** play with it?

12 **Write clues about these inventions.**

1. knife (cut meat) _You cut meat with it. You hold it in your hand._

2. rubber (rub out writing) _____

3. rucksack (carry things) _____

4. mobile phone (make calls) _____

13 **Play a game.** Work with a friend. Ask questions about the inventions you see. Take turns.

Heads = 1 space

Tails = 2 spaces

What's this?

It's an umbrella.

How do you use it?

You put it over your head when it's raining.

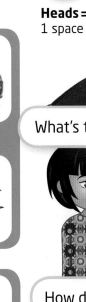

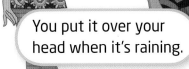

Creative Kids

Did you know that a teenager had the first idea for a television? And a six-year-old boy invented the toy lorry? Young people are great inventors because they have a lot of creativity and imagination.

1994: Chris Haas was nine years old when he designed a '**hands-on basketball**.' His basketball has painted hands on it. The hands show you where to put *your* hands when you throw the ball. Chris had the idea when he saw his friends miss lots of baskets. Today people use his invention around the world.

1994: '**Wristies**'™ protect you from the cold. You wear them under your coat and gloves in winter. Kathryn Gregory was only ten when she had the idea. She was in the snow and her wrists hurt because they were cold and wet. So she invented Wristies. Today millions of people use Wristies.

1905: When Frank Epperson was eleven, he left a cup with some fizzy drink and a stick in his garden. That night he forgot about it. It was a very cold night. When he went outside the next morning he found something amazing: an **ice lolly**!

1825: Louis Braille had an accident when he was three. The accident left him blind. At that time, it was hard for blind children to read. They had to touch raised letters. But it was easy to confuse a Q with an O, an R with a B, and so on. When he was 15, Louis invented an alphabet that used raised dots. The **Braille** alphabet was a big success!

15 **Read and write.** Write the name of the invention.

1. It's something you eat. _____an ice lolly_____

2. It's useful for people who live in cold places. _____

3. It's something a blind person can use to read. _____

4. It's useful for basketball players. _____

5. It happened by accident. _____

16 **Read and write.** Complete the table.

Who?	When?	What?	Why?
Chris Haas	in 1994, when he was nine years old	a basketball	His friends missed lots of baskets.

17 **Work in groups of three.** Discuss the questions.
Have you got the same opinion?

Which story was the most interesting? Why?

Which invention was the most useful? Why?

NUMBER OF PATENT FILINGS AROUND THE WORLD

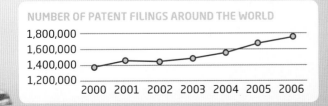

| | 2000 | 2001 | 2002 | 2003 | 2004 | 2005 | 2006 |

1,800,000
1,600,000
1,400,000
1,200,000

Weird but true

Diane Bisson, a Canadian industrial designer, invented a series of healthy and tasty plates and bowls that you can eat!

Paragraphs of Fact and Opinion

To introduce opinions, remember to use words like *in my opinion, I think* and *I believe*. A fact is a piece of true information, for example, a date, an event or a name. Use facts to support your opinions.

18 **Read.** Read this paragraph of fact and opinion. Underline facts that support the opinion.

A good idea

In my opinion, sticky notes are a great invention. They're a really good idea and they're easy to use. You lift the paper off, write a note and stick it on your notebook or on your computer. And they come off easily. I think most people like them *because they are so useful.* Before I started to use sticky notes, I used to forget everything!

I believe that the story of sticky notes is interesting, too. Sticky notes have two inventors. Spencer Silver invented the glue in 1970. It wasn't very strong. So he didn't know how he could use it. Four years later, Arthur Fry found a way to use the glue. One day, all his notes fell onto the floor. He wasn't happy! But he remembered Silver's glue. Later, he used the glue on small pieces of paper. It worked! The notes stayed on the paper and it was easy to remove them. And now we have a great – and useful – invention!

19 **Write.** Describe an invention. Explain how people use it and why you like it. Include facts to support your opinion.

20 **Work in groups of three.** Share your writing. Listen and write.

Invention	How do we use it?	Why does he/she like it?

Mission

Use your imagination and creativity to solve problems.

'In science it's always
a long train of ideas.
Many succeed, but in
between you often fail ...
science is entirely based
on curiosity.'

Aydogan Ozcan
Electrical Engineer
Emerging Explorer

- Work in a small group. What are some typical problems in your daily life? Discuss.

- Can you solve any of them with an invention? Share ideas for useful or fun inventions. Make notes.

I'd like to invent a flying machine.

- Work with another group. Share your ideas. Which inventions does everyone like best?

Plan an invention.

1. Choose a simple idea for an invention.

2. In small groups, draw or build your invention for a class science fair.

   a. Find the materials you need. If possible, recycle materials.

   b. Draw or build the invention.

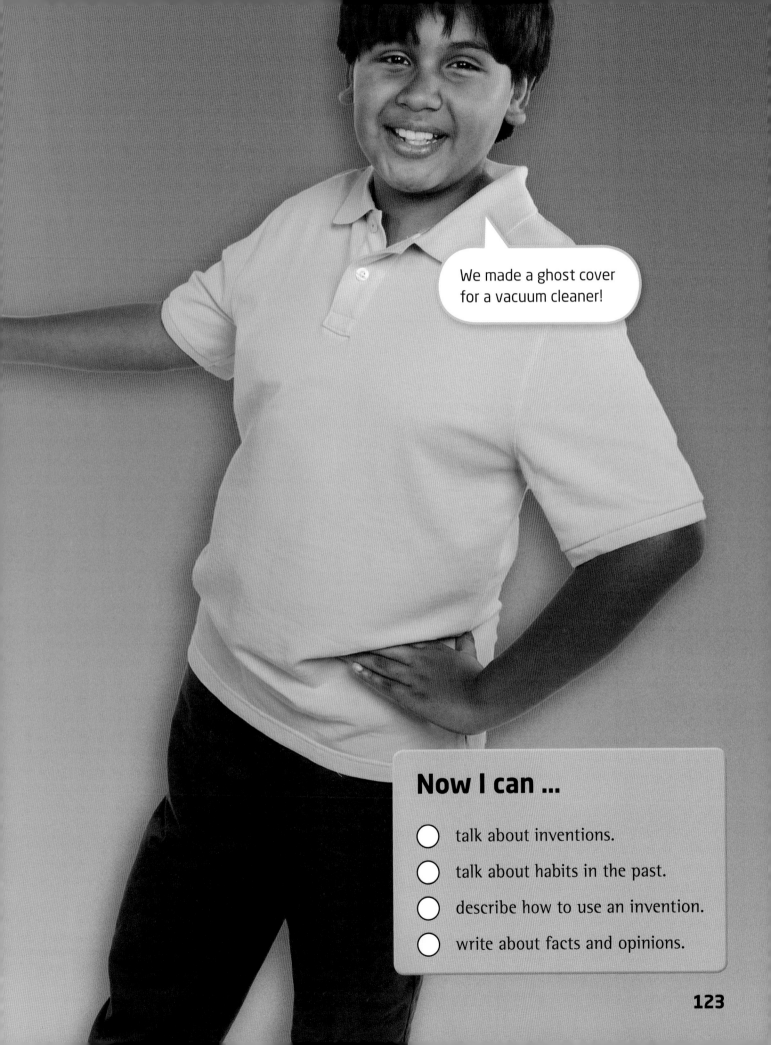

We made a ghost cover for a vacuum cleaner!

Now I can ...

- ⬤ talk about inventions.
- ⬤ talk about habits in the past.
- ⬤ describe how to use an invention.
- ⬤ write about facts and opinions.

That's Really Interesting!

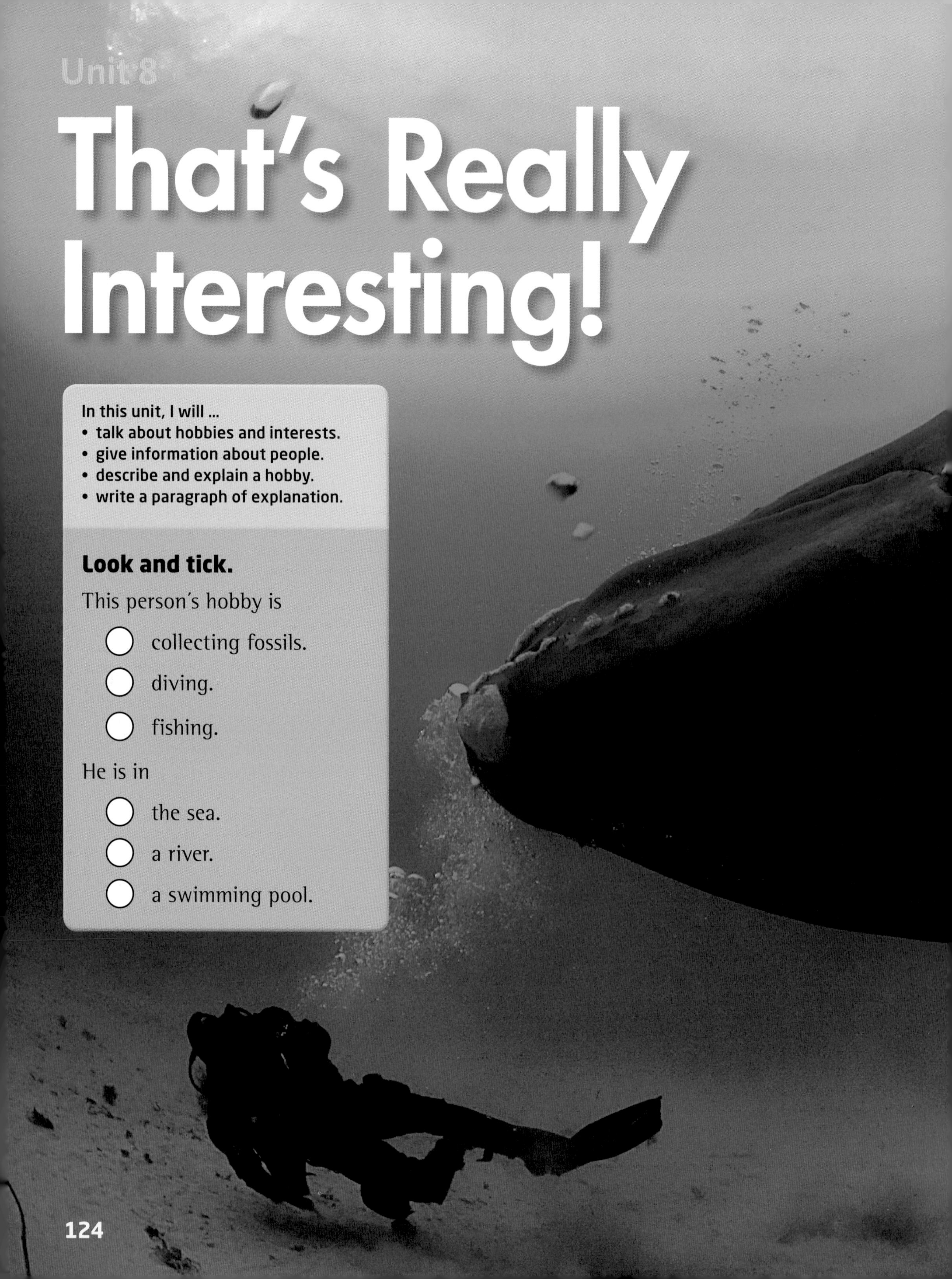

In this unit, I will …
- talk about hobbies and interests.
- give information about people.
- describe and explain a hobby.
- write a paragraph of explanation.

Look and tick.

This person's hobby is

- ◯ collecting fossils.
- ◯ diving.
- ◯ fishing.

He is in

- ◯ the sea.
- ◯ a river.
- ◯ a swimming pool.

Diver and southern right whale,
New Zealand

1 **Listen and read.** TR: B25

2 **Listen and repeat.** TR: B26

Most people have a hobby. Some children **collect** things, play in a **musical group** or grow vegetables. **Creative** people often paint or **take photos**. Computer games are popular, too. What hobbies do you **enjoy**?

take photos

collect

Many computer games are for one person. You play **alone**. But it's more fun to play with a friend. Choose your **avatars**. Then **compete**. To win the game, you must get lots of **points**. The person with the highest **score** wins.

In other computer games, you play **together** with a friend. You don't compete. You **co-operate**. When you use the **controllers**, you can see your avatars move on the **screen**.

an avatar

points

a score

a screen

9 13760

7831 7

a controller

3 **Work with a friend.**
What did you learn?
Ask and answer.

What do creative people do?

They often paint or take photos.

4 **Listen, read and sing.** TR: B27

What's Your Hobby?

What's your hobby?
What do you like doing?
What's your hobby?
I've got a hobby, too!

The boy who gets the highest score
wins the computer game.
The girl who collects fossils
wants to learn their names.
Who enjoys reading comics?
Who likes competing?
I collect soft toys
because I think they're sweet.

CHORUS

The boy who takes photos
sees them on the screen.
The girl who reads about dinosaurs
can see them in her dreams.
Do you like co-operating?
Do you like working alone?
I like talking about my hobby
on my new mobile phone.

It's fun being creative and showing what you can do.
Collecting, competing, co-operating.
I've got a hobby.
Have you?

CHORUS

5 **Work with a friend.** Answer.

1. Which hobbies are mentioned in the song?

2. Which of these hobbies do you like?

The person **who** has the highest score wins the game.
My friend **who** collects DVDs knows a lot about films.

6 **Read and write.** Join the two sentences.

1. I've got a younger brother. He loves computer games.

   I've got a younger brother who loves computer games.

2. There's a girl in my class. She collects seashells.

   _____

3. I like playing with other boys. They want to compete and win points.

   _____

4. My best friend is a creative person. She takes amazing photos.

   _____

5. I've got an aunt. She's very creative.

   _____

6. I've got two cousins. They collect fossils.

   _____

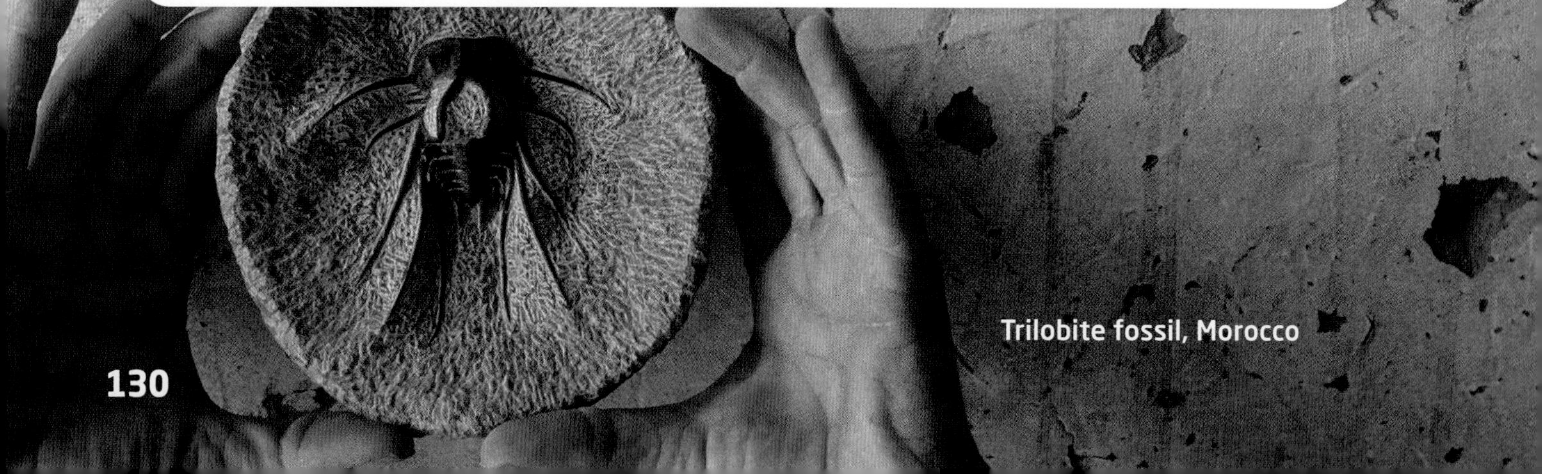

Trilobite fossil, Morocco

7 **What about you? Work in a group.** Ask questions. Write names. Then write about the people in your group on a sheet of paper.

Who . . .	Name(s)
1. enjoys books?	
2. likes competing in sports?	
3. likes playing computer games?	
4. often takes photos?	
5. has got more than one hobby?	
6. collects something?	

Sofia is someone who enjoys reading books.

8 **Read and talk.** Work in a new group. Read some of your sentences. Don't read the name. Can your group guess who it is?

This person is someone who enjoys reading books. Who is it?

Is it Tom?

No, it isn't. Try again!

9 **Listen and repeat.** Tick **T** for *True* or **F** for *False*. TR: B29

a comic

an insect

a fossil

a dinosaur

a soft toy

1. She's scared of insects. (T) (F)

2. She thinks dinosaurs are boring. (T) (F)

3. She knows a boy who collects comics. (T) (F)

4. Her brother collects fossils. (T) (F)

5. Her dad gave her a soft toy for her birthday. (T) (F)

10 **Work with a friend.** It's party time.
What present did you give? Stick.
Ask and answer.

> What did you give Maria?

> I gave her a pair of socks.

> How boring! I gave her a doll!

1   2   3   4   5

My dad gave <u>this fossil</u> **to me**. = My dad gave **me** <u>this fossil</u>.

My mum bought <u>soft toys</u> **for them**. = My mum bought **them** <u>soft toys</u>.

Show <u>the comic</u> **to James**. = Show **James** <u>the comic</u>.

11 **Read and write.** Rewrite the sentences.

1. When my brother was in the hospital, my uncle gave a soft toy to him.

   When my brother was in the hospital, my uncle gave him a soft toy.

2. My cousin sent a dinosaur book to him.

   _____

3. He became friends with two children and gave two comics to them.

   _____

4. Grandma sent a present to him, and he wrote a letter to her.

   _____

12 **Play a game.** Cut out the game board and the cube on page 171. Work with a friend. Take turns.

me = 1 space ☺
him/her/them = 0 spaces ☹

My friend gave me a toy dinosaur!

Yes, he gave a toy dinosaur to me.

Really?

Hide and Seek

'Letterboxing' is a fun outdoor hobby. Here's how it works: people hide a box. Inside the box, they put a rubber stamp and a notebook. They post clues on websites to help you find the box.

Then you look for the letterbox! You need to have your internet clues, a pen or pencil, your notebook and a rubber stamp. You may need a map and compass, too.

When you find the letterbox, you look for the notebook inside. Then, you write your name, home town and the date. You press your rubber stamp on the page. Then you take the stamp from inside the box and stamp it in your own notebook. Finally, you wrap the box carefully. You leave it where you found it for another person to find.

Dorrie and her mum love letterboxing! On their last holiday, they used clues to find a letterbox. Her mum read one clue: 'Pass the apple tree on your right.' Then she read the last clue: 'Keep your back to the tree and take four steps.' Dorrie took four steps. There it was! It was a plastic box, hidden under some stones. Dorrie read the notebook to see who was there before her. She added her name and stamp and then used the stamp from the letterbox on her notebook.

Dorrie wants to go letterboxing again. She says, 'I love reading mysteries and solving problems!'

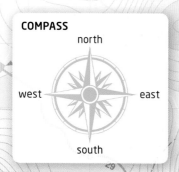

COMPASS
north
west • east
south

Weird but true

A Japanese sailor sent a message in a bottle when his boat was sinking. The message asked for help. About 150 years later, the bottle arrived in the town where he was born!

14 **Read.** Put the letterboxing steps in order.

_____ You write in and stamp the notebook.

_____ You find a notebook and a rubber stamp in a box.

_____ When you finish, you take your rubber stamp back with you.

_____ Then, you press the letterbox stamp on your notebook.

_____ You open it.

15 **Write.** Label the pictures.

> **a.** map   **b.** ~~rubber stamp~~   **c.** notebook   **d.** water bottle
>
> **e.** letterbox website   **f.** compass   **g.** clue   **h.** pen/pencil

b ☐   ☐   ☐   ☐

☐   "Keep your back to the tree and take four steps."   ☐   ☐

16 **Work in a group.** Discuss what people should take with them when they go letterboxing. Write your ideas in the table.

Very important	Important	Not important

Paragraphs of Explanation

In a paragraph of explanation, you describe something in general. You explain what it is and how you do it. You can explain difficult words and give examples. Use words and expressions like *for example* and *such as*.

17 **Read.** Read this paragraph of explanation. Underline definitions and examples.

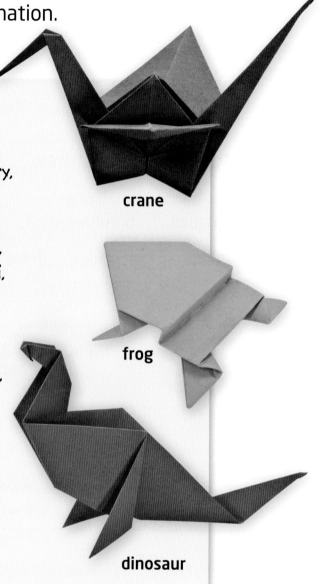

crane

frog

dinosaur

Fun with paper

Origami is a very popular hobby today. The Japanese invented it in the 17th century, and now it is famous everywhere in the world. The word 'origami' comes from two Japanese words: 'ori', which means 'folding', and 'kami', which means 'paper'. In origami, you always begin with one square sheet of paper. Then you fold the paper lots of times to make a shape. Origami is very creative. You can make very simple shapes, for example, a little insect. Or you can make a difficult design. To make a difficult shape, such as a dragon, you have to fold the paper lots of times in different ways. The most famous origami design is the Japanese paper crane. Origami can be more difficult than you think, but it's fun!

18 **Write.** Describe a hobby. Explain what it is and how you do it.

19 **Work in a group.** Share your writing. Listen and make notes.

136

NATIONAL GEOGRAPHIC

Mission

Enjoy a hobby.

'*As a child, I felt very alone with my interest in fossils. Finally, at age 13, I discovered there was a museum in Norway that actually employed people to study fossils.*'

Jørn Hurum, Palaeontologist
Emerging Explorer

- **Work with a friend. Why is it good to have a hobby? Discuss.**

- **What hobby would you like to try? Think of ideas. Make notes.**

I'd like to play in a band.

- **Work with a group. Share your ideas. Are they the same or different? Which ideas does everyone like best?**

Ammonite fossils

20 **Present a hobby.**

1. Research some hobbies and interests.
2. Decide on one hobby or interest.
3. Prepare a report for the class.
    a. Explain details about it.
    b. Explain how you do it.
    c. Use drawings or photos.

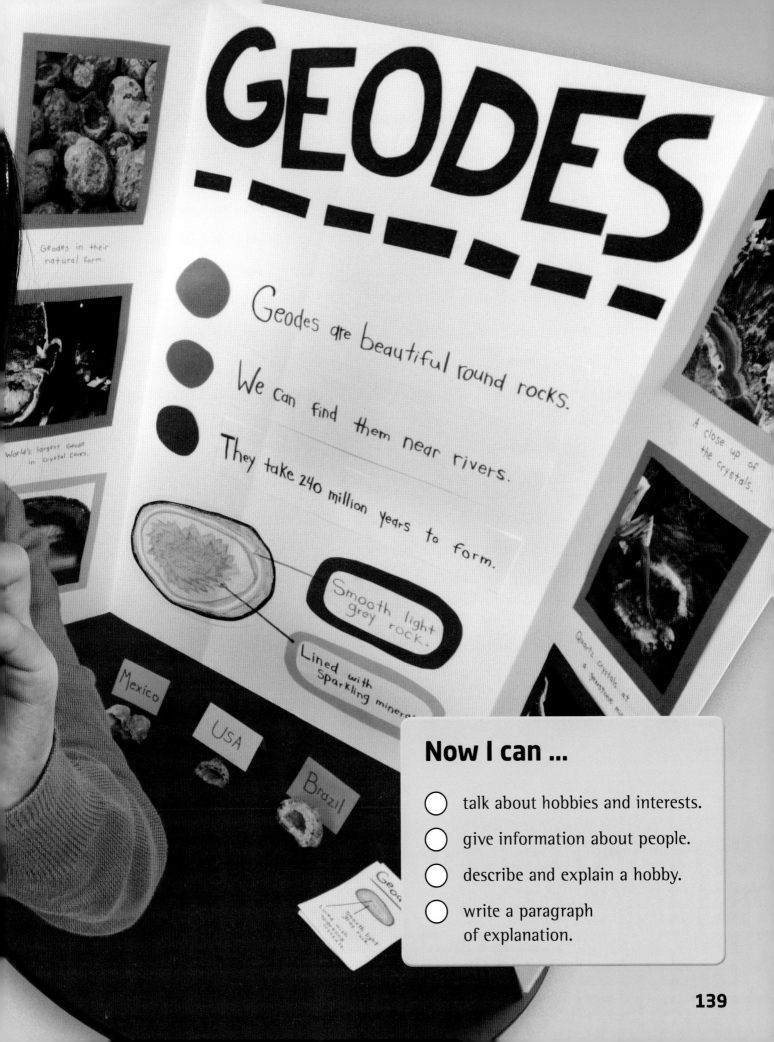

GEODES

Geodes are beautiful round rocks.

We can find them near rivers.

They take 240 million years to form.

Geodes in their natural form.

World's largest Geode in Crystal Caves.

A close up of the crystals.

Quartz crystals at a gemstone m

Smooth light grey rock.

Lined with sparkling minera

Mexico

USA

Brazil

Geo

Now I can ...

○ talk about hobbies and interests.

○ give information about people.

○ describe and explain a hobby.

○ write a paragraph of explanation.

The Science of Fun

In this unit, I will ...
- identify actions which use force.
- understand and make definitions.
- read a text and retell the information.
- write a paragraph of cause and effect.

Look and answer.

1. What is he doing?

2. Is it easy?

3. Write a caption for the photo.

_____

Chamonix, France

1 **Listen and read.** TR: 032

2 **Listen and repeat.** TR: 033

We use **force** to move. Force **happens** when we **push** or **pull**. Do you push or pull when you move on a **swing**? You do both.

Look at this **skater**. To move, skaters push on the ice. A push can move a skater **forwards**. It can also move a skater **backwards**.

forwards

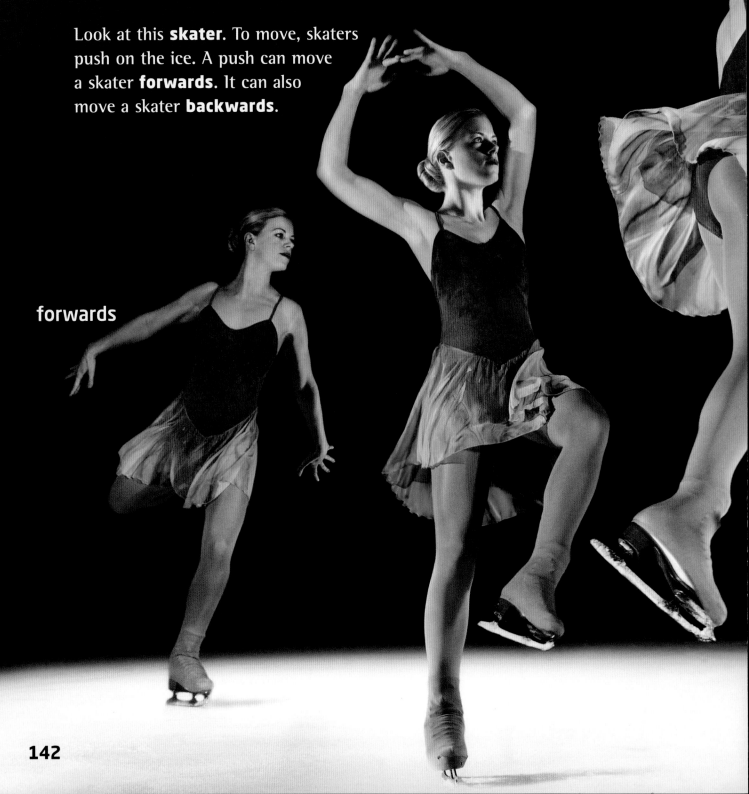

Skaters pull, too. Look at these skaters. The more one skater pulls, the more they **spin**. The skaters don't **fall over** because they know how to **balance**.

skaters

How do skaters stop? They use force. Skaters **push down** hard on their skates. The skates **connect** with the ice. The ice and skates **rub** together. When two things rub together, it's called **friction**.

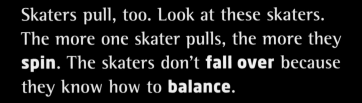

backwards

3 **Work with a friend.** What did you learn? Ask and answer.

How do skaters stop?

They use force.

4 **Listen, read and sing.** TR: B34

I'm on the Move!

Push it! Pull it! Push it! Pull it! Push! Pull!
Push! Pull! Push! Pull! Watch it go!

If you spin round and round, and round and round,
a force is what you feel.
If you fall down, down, down, down,
down to the ground,
that's gravity, of course.

I have to move.
I have to move.
It's amazing what you can do
when you let force do the work for you!

The more you push, the faster some things move.
When you spin round, a force comes and goes.

CHORUS

The more you push, the faster some things move.
When you spin round, a force comes and goes.

Push it! Pull it! Push it! Pull it! Push! Pull!
Push! Pull! Push! Pull! Watch it go!

If you spin round and round, and round and round,
a force is what you feel.
If you fall down, down, down, down,
down to the ground,
that's gravity, of course.

CHORUS

I have to move!

5 **Work with a friend.** Answer.

1. How do you feel when you spin?
   And when you fall?

2. Look at the photo. Is he pushing or pulling?

144

Tennessee, USA

The **more** one skater pulls, **the more** the other one spins.
The **more** force you use, **the faster** you go.
The **more** difficult the jump, **the more** practice you need.

6 **Match the pictures to the first part of the sentences.**
Then match to complete the sentences.

The more they spin,   the higher he goes.

The more she pushes,   the higher she goes.

The more he pushes down,   the faster they go.

7 **Read and write.**
Complete the sentences.

1. The more he goes down, _____ *the more she goes up.* _____

2. The more she goes up, _____.

3. The more he goes round, _____.

4. The more she spins, _____.

146

8 **Read and write.** Complete the sentences. Match them to the picture.

1. _____*The more she pushes*_____ (she / push) on the swing,

_____*the higher she goes*_____. (high / she / go)

2. _____, (the skateboarder / push)

_____. (he / move / forwards)

3. _____, (he / spin)

_____. (he / feel dizzy)

4. _____, (you / play football)

_____. (good / you / get)

9 **Work with a friend.** Imagine you are having fun. Describe what happens to you.

ball	football	good	high	fast
force	climb	jump	play	laugh
	push	pull	practise	win	

> The more you play, the more you laugh!

> The more you practise, the faster you run!

147

10 **Listen and repeat.** Read and write. Complete the sentences. TR: B36

towards

direction

away from

lean

gravity

1. When you throw a ball, _____ pulls it towards the Earth.

2. Don't go in that _____. Turn left!

3. He is walking _____ the music because it's too loud.

4. When you ride your bicycle and want to turn left, you turn your wheels to

the left, and you _____ to the left.

5. She is riding _____ the swings because she wants
to play on them.

11 **Listen and stick.** Work with a friend. Compare your answers. TR: B37

| 1 | 2 | 3 | 4 | 5 |

The force **which** pulls you towards the centre of the Earth is called gravity.
Skates are special shoes **which** you wear when you go ice skating.

12 **Write a definition for each item.** Work with a friend.
Read your definitions and guess. Take turns.

1. Bicycle: This is a machine _with wheels which you can ride in the park._

2. Skateboarding: It is a hobby _____.

3. Friction: This is a force _____.

4. Snakes and ladders: It is a game _____.

5. Football: This is a sport _____.

13 **Play a game.** Play with a friend. Cut out the cards on page
173. Follow the instructions. Take turns.

= Pick up a card.

A bicycle is a machine with wheels and handlebars which you ride.

OK! My turn!

Up, Down and All Around!

You are going on a roller-coaster ride. Sit in the car and pull down the safety bar. Are you ready? Let's go!

First, you go up a steep hill. The roller coaster goes slowly. Next, gravity pulls you down the hill. The roller coaster moves quickly. You feel very light!

A big circle, known as the 'loop-the-loop', is many people's favourite. When you go quickly up the circle, you feel heavy. Gravity is pulling you down. When you reach the top, you are high in the sky. And you're hanging upside down! So why don't you fall out of your seat? Your body wants to fly off, but the speed of the car and a force called centripetal force keep you moving in a circle, and keep you in your seat!

The roller coaster uses friction to stop. If it stops quickly, your body wants to continue moving. That is called inertia. But the safety bars keep you in place!

Not everyone loves roller coasters. They make some people feel dizzy or sick because the forces change. In fact, we experience forces like friction, centripetal force and gravity every day. For example, you feel gravity when you jump with your bike and come down. You feel centripetal force when you turn and you feel friction when you use the brakes to stop the bike.

How do you want to experience the forces? Do you want to ride your bicycle or a roller coaster?

The Russians invented the roller coaster. They made the 'cars' from ice. And they put fur on the seats to keep the passengers warm.

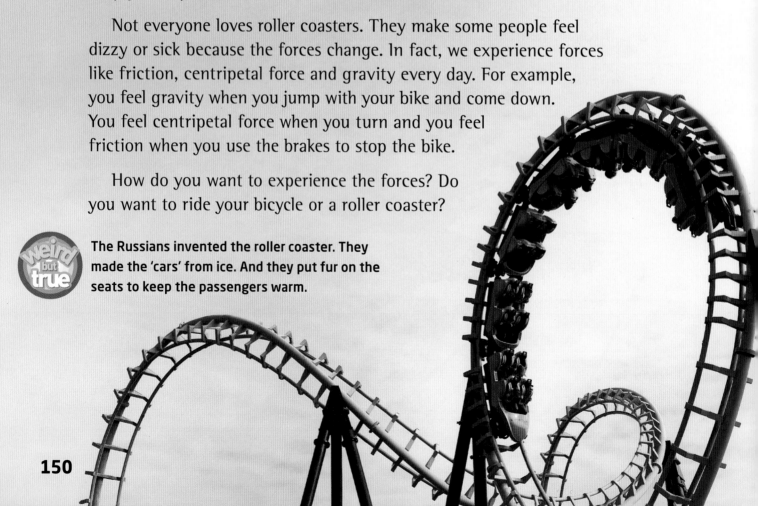

15 **Work with a friend.** Answer the questions.

1. What is the first thing you do when you sit in a roller coaster?

2. How do you feel when you go quickly down the hill?

3. How do you feel when you go quickly up the loop-the-loop?

4. Why do some people feel dizzy or sick on roller coasters?

16 **Complete the table.** Work with a friend. When do you experience these forces in roller coasters and bicycles?

	Roller coaster	Bicycle
Gravity		
Centripetal force		
Friction		
Inertia		

17 **Look and discuss.** Work with a friend. Describe a ride on a roller coaster.

What does the roller coaster look like?

It looks like a spaceship!

What happens first?

You go straight towards a moon, but then you turn!

Paragraphs of Cause and Effect

In a paragraph of cause and effect, you describe actions and say why they happened. You also describe the effect of the action. To show effect, you use words like *so*, *so that* and *as a result*.

18 **Read.** How does the writer describe cause and effect? Underline the words and phrases.

Last week, I learnt how to play tetherball with my brother. It's great. Two people play the game. One person hits the ball to the right. The other person hits it to the left. The ball is connected to a rope so that it doesn't fly away. To win, you have to hit the ball so that it turns round and round the pole! Tetherball looks easy, but it isn't. Every time I hit the ball, it flew up in a big circle. So it was easy for my brother to hit it! My brother is better than I am. First, he hit the ball and then he pushed it with his hands. When he hit the ball, it went round the pole. As a result, he won every game! I want to play again soon, but not with my brother!

19 **Write.** Describe a game or an activity. Include words of cause and effect.

20 **Work with a group.** Listen to the descriptions. Make notes.

Name	Game or activity	How to do or play it

NATIONAL GEOGRAPHIC

Mission

Think creatively and critically.

'When something unexpected or unusual happens, I am always curious to find out why.'

Stephon Alexander
Theoretical Physicist
Emerging Explorer

- Work with a group. Why is it important to understand how and why things work? Discuss.

- How can we learn more about how and why things work? Share your ideas. Write the best ideas in the box.

We can look in books or on the Internet.

_____

_____

_____

_____

_____

- Join another group. Share your ideas. Are they the same or different? Which ideas does everyone like best?

Spiral galaxy, photographed
from Hubble Space Telescope

21 Reinvent the wheel.

1. Work in small groups and research something you would like to make.

2. Collect all the things you need to make the object.

3. Join another group and show them what you have made. Explain how it works.

4. Discuss what you can do to make it better. Try it again!

Now I can ...

◯ identify actions which use force.

◯ understand and make definitions.

◯ read a text and retell the information.

◯ write a paragraph of cause and effect.

I'm using wheels to decorate paper.

Review

1 **Listen.** Tick the inventions that you hear. TR: B40

☐ aeroplane   ☐ battery   ☐ rubber   ☐ wheel

2 **Listen again.** Answer the questions. TR: B41

1. How many points have Anya and Ben got at the beginning? _____

2. What was Charles Goodyear's idea? _____

3. What is Anya's score at the end of the competition? _____

4. What will Anya do next month? _____

3 **Work with a friend.** Take turns. Ask and answer questions about life before these inventions.

How did people use to tell the time before they had clocks?

They used to look at the Sun.

That's right.

4 **Read and write.**

a dinosaur	fail	a hobby	an inventor
a skater	swings	together	towards

1. This is a person who moves, turns and spins on ice. _____

2. Collecting fossils is an example of this. _____

3. This is a person who invents things. _____

4. This is a creature which lived millions of years ago. _____

5. It's the opposite of *alone*. _____

6. It's the opposite of *away from*. _____

7. The more you push these, the higher they go. _____

8. You can try again when this happens. _____

5 **Work with a friend.** Choose list A, B or C.
Write definitions in your notebook.

A	**B**	**C**
an avatar	an insect	backwards
a battery	electricity	gravity
a comic	a good friend	a screen
a creative person	a problem	a soft toy
(to) pull	a wheel	(to) take photos

It's the opposite of push.

It's the force that pulls
you towards the Earth.

6 **Work in a group.** Take turns. Read your definitions to the
others. Can they guess?

Let's Talk

Wow, that's cool!

I will ...
- ask questions.
- show I'm interested.
- keep the conversation going.

1 Listen and read. TR: B42

Pablo: What's your favourite sport?

Mario: Football. I want to be a professional football player.

Pablo: **Do you?**

Mario: Yes! **What about you?** What's your favourite sport?

Pablo: I love football, too. My dad's taking me to the World Cup!

Mario: Wow. **That's amazing!**

Do you? (Can you? / Are you?) Really? Wow.	**What about you?** How about you? And you?	That's great! **That's amazing!** How cool!

2 Work with a friend. Use the table. Talk about your favourite hobby or person.

What does that mean?

I will …
- interrupt someone (formally and informally).
- ask the meaning and ask how to spell or say something.
- explain a meaning and give a spelling.
- say that I don't know.

3 **Listen and read.** TR: B43

Antoni: **Hey**, Martina, **what does this mean?**

Martina: **I don't know. I think it's a kind of** invention.

Antoni: Er, I don't think so.

Martina: Why don't you ask the teacher?

Antoni: **That's a good idea. Excuse me**, Mrs Biga.
What does this word mean?

Hey, Excuse me, Mr / Ms / Mrs _____.	What does _____ mean?	**I think it's a kind of** _____. I think it means _____. It's the opposite of _____.	**I don't know.** I'm not sure.	**That's a good idea.** Good point.
	How do you spell _____? How do you pronounce this word? How do you say _____?			

4 **Listen.** You will hear two discussions. Read each question and circle the answer. TR: B44

1. What does the boy want to know?
   a. meaning   b. spelling   c. pronunciation

2. What does the girl want to know?
   a. meaning   b. spelling   c. pronunciation

5 **Work in pairs.** Prepare and practise discussions. You want to know the spelling, the meaning or the pronunciation of a word. Ask your friend and then ask the teacher.

Irregular Verbs

Infinitive	Past Simple	Past Participle	Infinitive	Past Simple	Past Participle
be	was/were	been	lie	lay	lain
beat	beat	beaten	light	lit	lit
become	became	become	lose	lost	lost
begin	began	begun	make	made	made
bend	bent	bent	meet	met	met
bite	bit	bitten	pay	paid	paid
bleed	bled	bled	put	put	put
blow	blew	blown	read	read	read
break	broke	broken	ride	rode	ridden
bring	brought	brought	ring	rang	rung
build	built	built	rise	rose	risen
buy	bought	bought	run	ran	run
catch	caught	caught	say	said	said
choose	chose	chosen	see	saw	seen
come	came	come	sell	sold	sold
cost	cost	cost	send	sent	sent
cut	cut	cut	set	set	set
dig	dug	dug	sew	sewed	sewn
do	did	done	shake	shook	shaken
draw	drew	drawn	shine	shone	shone
drink	drank	drunk	show	showed	shown
drive	drove	driven	shut	shut	shut
eat	ate	eaten	sing	sang	sung
fall	fell	fallen	sink	sank	sunk
feed	fed	fed	sit	sat	sat
feel	felt	felt	sleep	slept	slept
fight	fought	fought	slide	slid	slid
find	found	found	speak	spoke	spoken
fly	flew	flown	spend	spent	spent
forget	forgot	forgotten	spin	spun	spun
forgive	forgave	forgiven	stand	stood	stood
freeze	froze	frozen	steal	stole	stolen
get	got	got	stick	stuck	stuck
give	gave	given	sting	stung	stung
go	went	gone	stink	stank	stunk
grow	grew	grown	sweep	swept	swept
hang	hung	hung	swim	swam	swum
have	had	had	swing	swung	swung
hear	heard	heard	take	took	taken
hide	hid	hidden	teach	taught	taught
hit	hit	hit	tear	tore	torn
hold	held	held	tell	told	told
hurt	hurt	hurt	think	thought	thought
keep	kept	kept	throw	threw	thrown
know	knew	known	understand	understood	understood
learn	learnt	learnt	wake up	woke up	woken up
leave	left	left	wear	wore	worn
lend	lent	lent	win	won	won
let	let	let	write	wrote	written

| after lunch | after school | tonight |
| on Saturday | before school | after dinner |

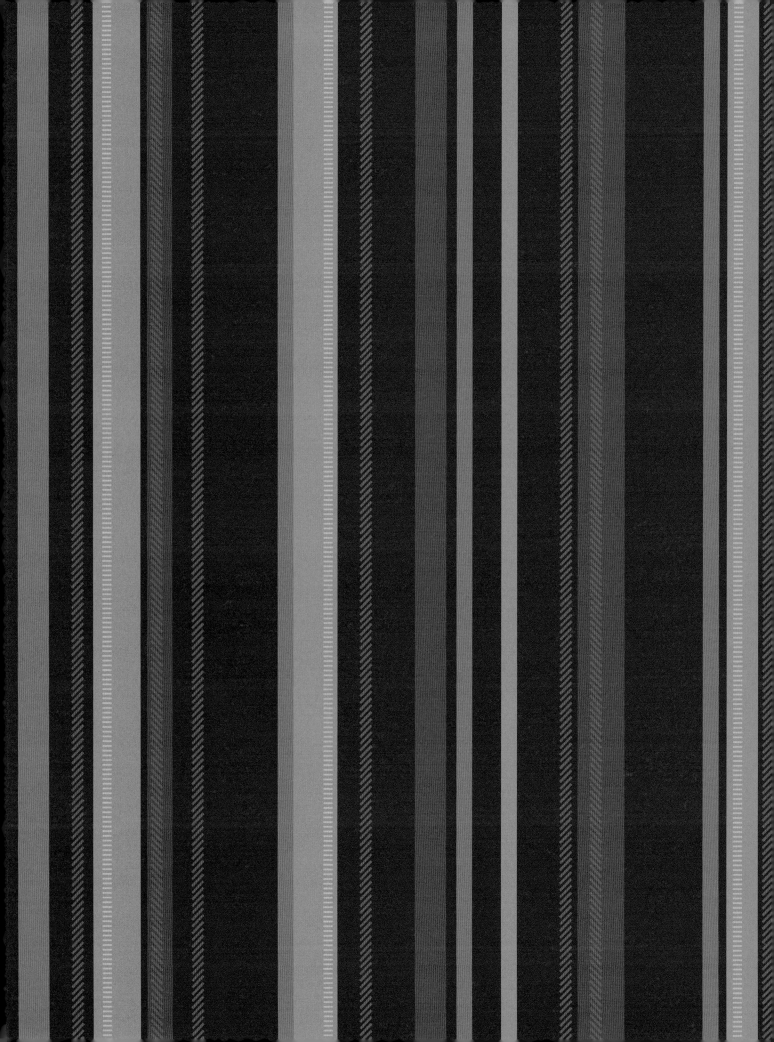

End

There is no electricity. Go back two spaces.

You have to wash clothes by hand. Go back one space.

Start

a famous person	a sport	interesting	good
food	a writer / book	cool	bad
a computer game	a hobby	boring	amazing
a school subject	music / a song	wonderful	popular

	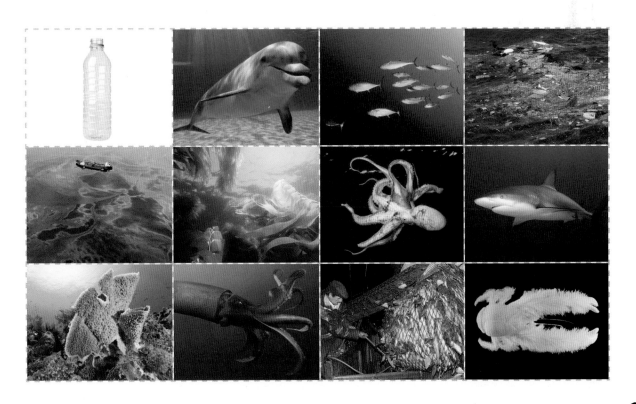		**biodegradable**
must			
	will		

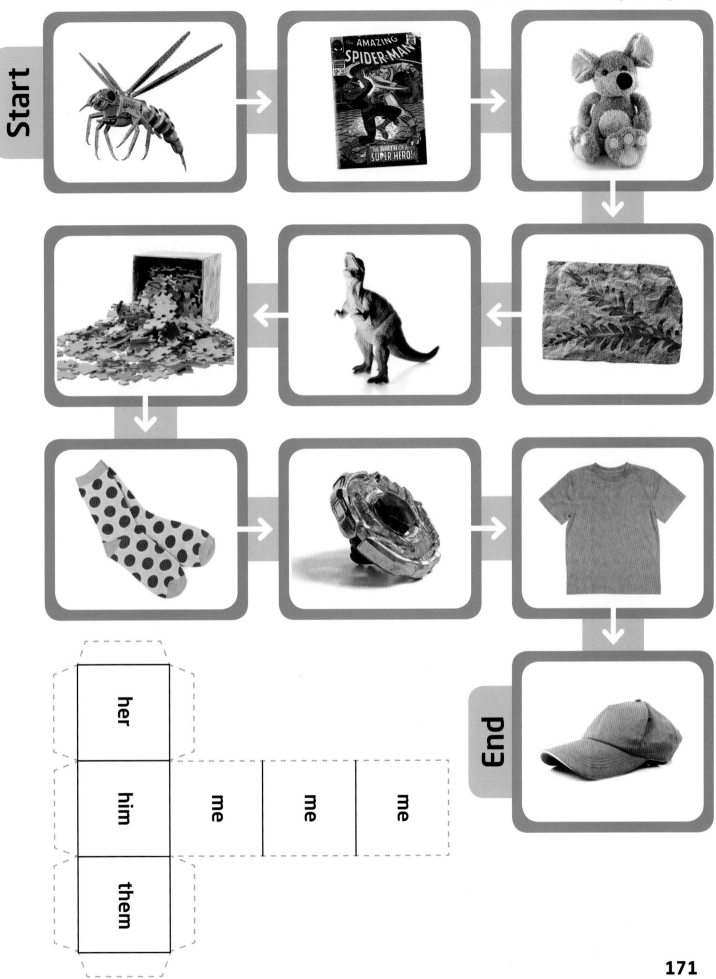

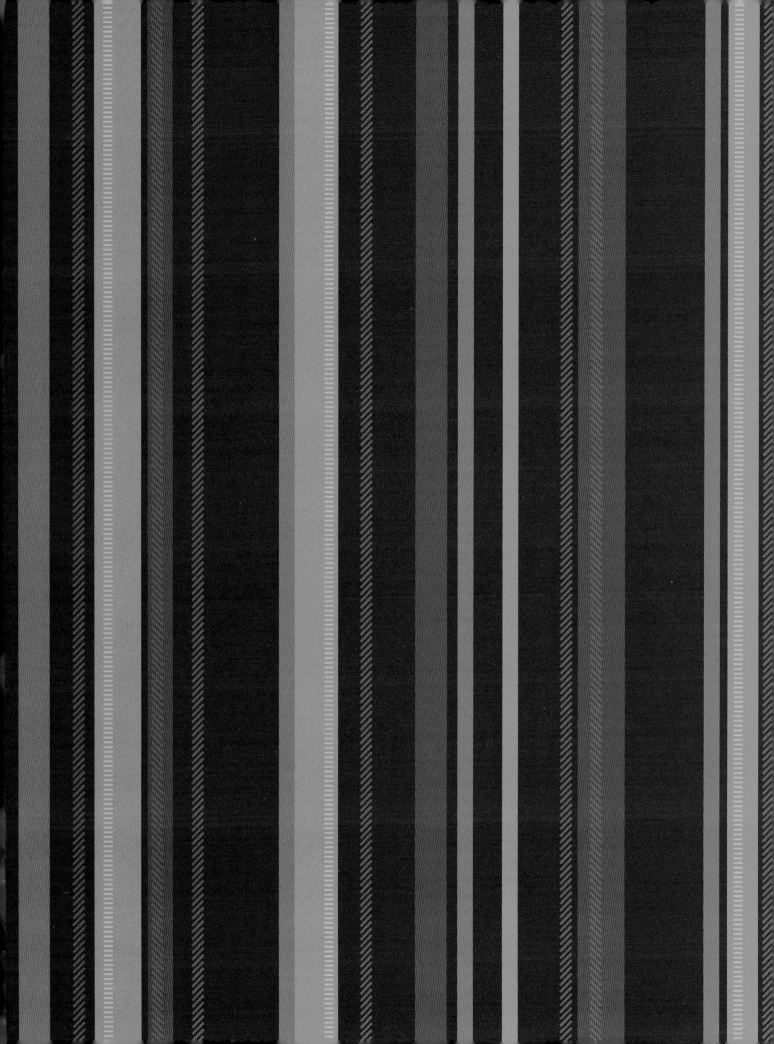

12

What is a bicycle?
(a machine / wheels
and handlebars /
which / ride)

19

This is a force
which pulls you
to the Earth.
What is it?

27

This is a game
with a ball which
you play in the
garden. What is it?

34

This is a force which
happens when two
things rub together.
What is it?

10

Act out: 'pull'

16

What is a
skateboard?
(a board with
wheels / which /
move on)

25

What is a
mobile phone?
(a thing / which /
use / talk)

32

What is a hobby?
(a thing / which /
do / spare time)

4

This is a playground
object which goes up
and down. What is it?

14

Act out: 'spin'

24

Act out:
'lose your balance'

30

Act out: 'push'